Team Launch!

Strategies for
New Team
Start-Ups

Team Leader's Manual

Written by

Ingrid Bens, M.Ed.

Team Launch!

Strategies for New Team Start-Ups: Team Leader's Manual

Development Team

Writer
Ingrid Bens, M.Ed.

Editor
Michael Goldman

Revisions
Dan Picard

Cover
Michele Kierstead

Typography
Mary House

GOAL/QPC

2 Manor Parkway, Salem, NH 03079-2841

Toll free: 800-643-4316   **Phone:** 603-890-8800
Fax: 603-870-9122   **E-mail:** service@goalqpc.com
Web site: www.goalqpc.com

Printed in the United States of America
First Edition
9 8 7 6 5 4 3 2 1
ISBN 1-57681-036-4
(Previously published by Participative Dynamics, ISBN 1-890416-01-0)

So, You've Been Asked to Lead a Team!

*E*very year, thousands of experienced supervisors and managers like you are asked to become team leaders. If you've been in a supervisory or managerial position for a while, you're probably wondering:

> • *How is being a team leader going to be different from supervising a work group?*
> • *How is a team different from any other staff group?*
> • *What do I have to do differently to lead this team?*

You may even be thinking that because you've chaired project teams and held meetings, this "team thing" isn't going to be anything new...*or is it?*

In fact, building and leading a team is significantly different from managing other groups. Even if you have had years of experience with projects and committees, the implementation of an empowered work team will represent a major change, not only for you as the leader but for the team's members as well.

This workbook has been written after a decade of experience helping leaders build and nurture new teams. It answers many of the most common questions leaders have and provides a step-by-step process for establishing a new team.

Over the years we have learned about the dangers of jumping into teamwork without laying a proper foundation. Like a house without solid footings, teams that are started without a careful formation process will eventually crumble and fall. We don't want that to happen to your team!

Instead, we want you to start your new team with a clear understanding of how teams operate and what they need to get off to a strong start. We will provide you with a definition of teams in the context of today's trends, and describe how teams are different from other groups.

The unique feature of this workbook is that it lays out step-by-step instructions for the launch meeting of your new team. These instructions include detailed notes about how to run that crucial first session and worksheets for facilitating discussions.

This manual has a companion workbook for members called *Team Launch! Team Member's Manual* (contact GOAL/QPC at www.goalqpc.com to order).

This workbook is the first of a two-part series. Each book addresses one of the two most challenging stages of team development: *Team Launch!* addresses challenge #1, which is getting your team off to a solid start. *Advanced Team Facilitation* focuses on challenge #2, which is dealing with the "storming" phase of team development, when conflict so often derails productivity. Contact GOAL/QPC for information about ordering these books and additional resources about teaming.

We know from our experience in helping hundreds of team leaders just like you that you will find these two workbooks to be tremendously helpful in planning for and leading your team to success.

Best wishes for a successful team launch!

Ingrid Bens, M.Ed.

Some Definitions

Facilitator:
One who contributes *structure* and *process* to interactions so groups are able to function effectively and make high-quality decisions. A helper and enabler whose goal is to support others as they achieve exceptional performance.

Content:
The topics or subjects under discussion at any meeting. Also referred to as the task, the decisions made, or the issues explored.

Process:
The structure, framework, methods, and tools used in interactions. Refers to the climate or spirit established, as well as the style of the facilitator.

Intervention:
An action or set of actions that aims to improve the functioning of a group.

Plenary:
A large group session held to share the ideas developed in separate subgroups.

Norms:
A set of rules created by group members with which they mutually agree to govern themselves.

Group:
A collection of individuals who come together to share information, coordinate their efforts, or achieve a task, but who mainly pursue their own individual goals and work independently.

Team:
A group of individuals who are committed to achieving a common goal, who support each other, who fully utilize member resources, and who have closely linked roles.

Table of Contents

Table of Contents

Why Teams Now?

You have probably noticed that more and more organizations are turning to teams these days.

When organizations seriously started using teams during the sixties and seventies, they were often formed to handle special projects such as the development of a new product or the creation of a new production line. The regular work of the organization was done in functional departments, where the real authority lay. Committees and teams were seen as special purpose bodies, formed to carry out specific tasks that required cross-functional or cross-departmental cooperation.

During the 1980s there was a sudden increase in the use of teams as organizations woke up to the need to focus on Quality. By mid-decade, tens of thousands of Quality Circles had sprung up all across North America, especially in the manufacturing sector.

The eighties also saw a general increase in the number and variety of task forces and committees. In both the public and private sectors, teams became a way of doing everything from improving customer service and simplifying processes, to handling important new business initiatives. In a hierarchical world of multiple levels and separate functional departments, teams were recognized as an important means of connecting specialists and coordinating work between otherwise isolated departments.

Teams Inside a Hierarchical Organization

How the Role of Teams Is Changing

We all know that today's competitive pressures have forced every organization to reexamine its structure. Many have now realized that they can't afford to continue to operate with layer upon layer of management. To succeed in the future every enterprise has to be:

✔ Flatter, leaner, and much more flexible,

✔ Outward looking and focused on customers,

✔ Obsessed with excellence and continuous improvement,

✔ Able to get the most innovative ideas from all staff,

✔ Much faster in generating and implementing new ideas.

The organizational unit that most consistently delivers these advantages is a team. Instead of continuing to be organized by specialty departments like sales, accounting, and marketing, more and more organizations started to eliminate those departments throughout the 1990s and reorganize into teams based on a specific customer, product, or market segment. Today teams are becoming a fundamental organizational building block, instead of being used just for special projects.

The Benefits of Teams

This acceptance of teams comes after years of trials and pilot projects. The results have been assessed and the verdict is in… in the right environment, with proper training and adequate organizational support, teams are a superior way to organize work.

Among the documented benefits:

✔ Teams are more flexible than traditional departments and are better able to respond quickly to changing circumstances,

✔ Teams change the focus of employees, from satisfying the needs of people higher in the hierarchy to meeting the needs of customers,

✔ The synergy of teamwork creates better ideas than are generated by individuals working on their own,

✔ Teams that are built around key processes have a mandate to continuously improve what they are doing,

✔ There is often greater commitment and accountability because the goal of the team is created by its members,

✔ Teams bring together diverse skills and create a richer resource for the organization,

✔ Teams help create a learning culture,

✔ When employees are more empowered and accountable, it reduces the need for excessive management and supervision,

✔ Teams improve the bottom line.

This last point is of course *the* most compelling reason for implementing teams. Simply put, research has shown that over the past decade, those organizations that have implemented teams have gained significant competitive advantage over those that did not.

As a team leader, regardless of any other reasons, you need to always remember that your organization is implementing teams to improve the bottom line!

$Q.$ Which of the above benefits do you think your organization most wants to gain from your team?

_____

_____

_____

_____

_____

_____

_____

_____

_____

_____

_____

_____

How Teams Improve Profitability

There are <u>three</u> ways teams improve profitability:

1. Teams reduce the need for supervision. Many middle management and supervisory positions can be eliminated when employees become more self-managing.

2. Teams are more focused on serving the customer's needs than meeting the internal requirements of the organization. This gives teams a continuous improvement focus. Continuously improving customer contact and satisfaction ultimately improves the bottom line.

3. Teams support profitability by fostering creativity and innovation. If teams are properly staffed, adequately trained, and given enough autonomy, they have been proven to be superior to traditional departments in generating innovative, competitive ideas.

The Problem with Teams

In spite of their many advantages, every team leader needs to be aware of the disadvantages of teams. These include:

→ Teams have to meet often to even be a team. Finding time to meet in today's hectic work environment can be a real challenge that puts added pressure on everybody.

→ When teams find and solve problems, that activity generates action plans. These initiatives add extra work to everyone's already packed schedules. Although these improvements may ultimately save time, there is almost always a time crunch at the front end of team work.

→ Those people who prefer to work alone may resent being put on a team and/or hate going to meetings. Other people may have limited interpersonal skills and require a lot of coaching and training just to be able to get along.

→ Because teams emphasize consensus, decision making can be a slow and painful process, especially at the start when members are inexperienced.

→ Because there is a strong emphasis on interaction, teams demand that leaders and members spend a lot of time and effort on building relationships. This is new to many leaders and takes experience to do well.

→ Teams are hard on established career ladders because most traditional titles disappear. When everyone is a "colleague" or "associate" and there are no more levels to aspire to, some people lose their drive to succeed.

→ People who are used to competition with peers will find it hard to adjust to a more collaborative culture.

→ Once teams are established there are major challenges to link teams together and link team efforts to what is done in functional departments.

→ Leaders who are used to calling the shots often have a very hard time learning to let others make decisions. Leading a team requires a style shift. This is difficult for some new leaders.

→ Finally, the overall corporate culture may not be supportive of team decisions. Many companies think that they want teams, but actually have no desire or intention to really empower them enough to let them perform effectively.

In spite of all these blocks, the drive to build teams is accelerating and they will likely dominate the workplace in the decades ahead.

As a team leader you should expect that at least some of these blocks might manifest themselves in your situation. Anticipating blocks lets you create strategies to reduce their impact ahead of time.

Q. What do you expect will be the biggest blocks for your new team?

_____

_____

_____

_____

_____

_____

What Is a Team-Based Organization?

If you hear your organization announce that it's going to become team based, here is what that means:

✓ While some parts of the old hierarchical structure may remain, teams will be formed to manage most major products, processes, or market segments,

✓ All teams will be structured around either a customer, product, or service, and their related processes,

✓ Teams are being implemented as a strategic business decision – that is, to improve profitability,

✓ To stay relevant, team structures can be expected to change from time to time to keep pace with the shifting demands of the marketplace,

✓ People will be deployed to maximize their skills,

✓ Fewer people will be engaged in supervising and checking,

✓ The team will be expected to know its internal and external customer needs and continuously improve what they do to surpass customer expectations.

✓ Instead of rewarding employees for how many people they supervise, people will be paid on the basis of skills and their creative contribution to the bottom line,

✓ Team members will increasingly make the decisions previously made by managers and supervisors,

✓ The behavior of management will need to shift from command and control to facilitation and participation.

A team-based organization is basically one that has removed old departmental silos, reduced its hierarchical layers, and realigned employees to meet specific challenges.

While the outline of the hierarchy may still be present in a team-based organization, it no longer dictates priorities. Priorities are set by customers and the pressures of the global marketplace. Teams are formed to bring together the talents needed to satisfy these pressures.

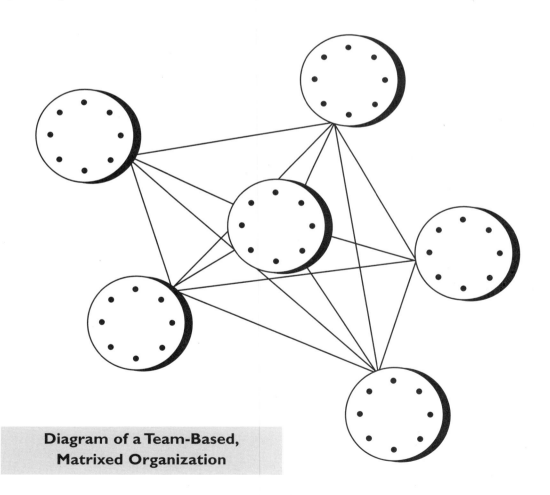

Diagram of a Team-Based, Matrixed Organization

How Is a Team-Based Organization Different from a Hierarchy?

Once the decision has been made to implement teams, the organization should be aware that it has made a commitment to abide by a number of fundamental principles. These include:

✓ More decisions (including many strategic ones) will be made by teams because they're closest to the customer or production point, rather than at management levels,

✓ Teams will need to be given considerable power to make decisions and implement change, which the organization will need to support, not block,

✓ Employees will increasingly turn to each other for advice, answers, and support, rather than go to supervisors or managers,

✓ A concerted effort has to be made to reduce bureaucracy and simplify processes, to speed up response times and innovation cycles,

✓ Operational excellence and superior customer service, rather than carrying out job-specific transactions, will be the focus of employee efforts,

✓ Everything will be open to continuous improvement; sacred cows ("that's how we always did it") will have to be sacrificed,

✓ There will be more job sharing, multi-skilling, and job redesign to fit situations, rather than structuring jobs to one specific task or specialty,

✓ Everyone must build in time to accommodate more meetings, more learning, more teaching, and coaching from leaders,

✓ Team members will monitor and report on their own and their team's progress, rather than expect evaluations to come "down" from above,

✓ Accountability for achieving goals will become a shared responsibility no longer strictly on the shoulders of managers.

The last point alludes to one of the major differentiators in a team world. In hierarchies, managers make decisions because they are accountable. In a team world, the leader and the members share accountability for their decisions and the impact those decisions have on the bottom line.

This shift in accountability is at the heart of the most difficult part of implementing teams — namely, creating a significant power shift from management to teams. Without this shift in power, implementing teams is largely a waste of both time and effort. This power shift affects both management as a group and individual team leaders who will need to learn to surrender power and play new roles.

If there is one recurring reason teams fail, it is that the host organization did not understand the dynamics of empowerment and failed to truly support teams to the extent that they should. An extensive exploration of empowerment begins on page 21 of this book.

Q. Which of the changes mentioned previously is going to be the hardest for you? For your organization?

_____

_____

_____

_____

_____

_____

_____

Know the Team Terminology

The following are terms that refer to the various types of teams. Some of these terms overlap because they refer to similar types of teams. Most organizations create their own terminology, so you may encounter a variety of interpretations of these terms.

Ad Hoc Groups	are informal groups that lack any real structure (i.e., a group that meets periodically to share information or liaise).
Intact or Functional Teams	are teams formed within a functional area. They are often made up of people with similar skills, led by a manager or supervisor (i.e., a staff team within a department).
Matrix or Cross-functional Teams	are teams of individuals with differing skills, drawn from across the organization (i.e., project or process improvement teams).
Semi-autonomous Teams	are formal teams that have been empowered to make some decisions on their own, but who for the most part require final approval before implementing the majority of their decisions. Matrix teams and functional work teams can both also be semi-autonomous (i.e., a semi-autonomous matrix team).
Autonomous or High Performance Teams	have achieved a state of independence and are empowered to implement the majority of their decisions without approval from senior levels. Autonomous teams often hire and fire their own members, manage their own budgets, and set their own work plans. These teams have high levels of autonomy to encourage creativity and innovation. Both functional teams and matrix teams can be established as autonomous teams (i.e., an autonomous matrix team).

Q. What terminology would you use to describe the type of team you'll be leading?

_____

_____

_____

Fundamental Team Design Principles

Regardless of the type of team or its responsibilities, all teams are essentially built on the same basic design principles and share this basic definition:

> *A team is a group of from four to fifteen individuals who are jointly accountable for a whole product, process, or specific customer. The members set their own goal, plan their own work, carry it out in a coordinated manner, and evaluate their own results.*

All true teams have:

✓ A common goal created by the members that supersedes the goals of each individual member,

✓ A set of specific objectives that describe how the team will achieve its goal, accompanied by specific performance targets,

✓ A clear set of rules known as "behavioral norms" created by the members,

✓ A strong focus on continuous improvement of all processes related to the product or service provided to the customer,

✓ A focus on solving problems and self-correcting internal team functions,

✓ Clearly defined accountabilities for all team outcomes,

✓ Specific levels of empowerment for each task to be undertaken by the team,

✓ Member control over most administrative functions of the team such as budgeting, work planning, and vacation scheduling,

✓ Highly developed interpersonal skills so teamwork is effective,

✓ An attitude that takes an assertive, problem-solving approach to conflict,

✓ Constant attention to training to increase member skills,

✓ A team leader who shares power, coaches, trains, and acts more like a facilitator than a traditional "boss,"

✓ Team members who are paid for their skills and their contribution to productivity, rather than their time,

✓ Regularly scheduled meetings (i.e., daily, weekly, biweekly, etc.) held frequently enough to provide continuity and momentum,

✓ Heightened levels of trust, candor, and caring among members,

✓ A "can do" attitude that grows out of commitment and having a say.

When to Use Teams

We all know that even a good thing can be misused. The logic goes that if teams are a good thing, then they should be created to do everything. This is mistaken thinking, because not all jobs are suited to teamwork.

It's important to remember that some situations are suitable for teams while others are not. A team should only be created when a specific performance objective requires a group effort and the application of multiple skills, perspectives, or experiences.

Even in an organization that has implemented teams everywhere, there will be some jobs that should remain in the hands of individuals working alone.

If you or your organization are wondering whether or not to create a team for a particular situation or task, here are some general rules of thumb:

Rely on individuals if:	Use teams if:
• There's a lack of time,	• The time needed for teamwork is available,
• The response is automatic,	• A creative response is important,
• One person is responsible,	• Responsibility should be shared,
• Information is available to only one person,	• Information can be shared with others,
• One perspective will suffice,	• Multiple perspectives are needed,
• One skill set is adequate,	• A range of skills must be applied,
• Membership will change,	• There will be a consistent group of people,
• There is no intention to empower.	• The members' empowerment levels will increase over time.

There are a lot of examples of teams that fizzle out because that particular group of people should never have been a team in the first place. When you are approached to start a team, ask yourself the following questions:

✓ *"Is there a good enough reason to get all these people together in the first place?"*

✓ *"Do we really have the time for all the meetings?"*

✓ *"Do we really need to think things out as a whole team?"*

✓ *"Is there a need to link our roles?"*

✓ *"Is a team really justified or should we simply be a less formal group?"*

✓ *"Will the organization truly empower the team?"*

Beware of the *bandwagon effect* – starting a team just for the sake of it. All team leaders need to remember that implementing teams is a business strategy designed to improve the bottom line. Teams are never an end in themselves, but a means of involving people in managing their piece of the business more effectively.

What Exactly Do Teams Do?

One of the most common misconceptions about teams is that teams actually carry out the work of the organization. Anyone who has ever tried to write a memo with the help of ten people knows firsthand how inefficient that is.

What teams actually do is think. Picture your team as a "collective brain" that comes together periodically to share ideas and make decisions. Once the decisions are made and the action plans are in place, the actual work of teams is conducted by individual members working alone or in small subgroups.

The chart that follows describes the approximate division of labor on any team.

Work together as a whole group to:
- Share information,
- Make decisions,
- Plan for action,
- Celebrate successes,
- Set goals and objectives,
- Coordinate member efforts,
- Find and solve problems,
- Learn new skills,
- Think of innovative approaches,
- Evaluate results,
- Give and receive feedback.

Use small subgroups to:
- Implement specific tasks or action steps that call for the efforts or ideas of more than one person.

Rely on individuals to:
- Conduct most other action steps created by the team,
- Perform specific jobs.

If you think of your team as a "thinking machine" whose output is ideas arrived at through collaboration, you won't make the mistake of asking the whole group to work on tasks better suited to individuals. Just remember that the actual work of any team is carried out by individual team members working alone or in small subgroups.

Q.   How clear do you think your team members are about whether they'll be working together or alone on most tasks?

_____
_____
_____
_____
_____
_____
_____

How Being on a Team Changes People's Jobs

When a new team is announced, prospective members often wonder how it's going to affect their daily routine. A common worry is that they'll have to give up their independence or the kind of work they've been used to doing. As a team leader you need to explore these concerns, one-on-one with each member before the team is launched, to answer questions and ease concerns.

How much being on a team will change people's jobs will also depend on the particulars of each situation. Some people will end up working on one team while still working in their old "home" department. Others will be placed on two teams and will no longer work in a home department.

Example 1: Joe is part of a matrix team to improve on-time delivery to a key customer. Joe attends two two-hour meetings per week with this team. He spends an additional sixteen hours a week carrying out the task decided on by that team. The rest of the time, Joe is still a member of the Purchasing Department, where he handles large capital tenders. Joe's time is therefore 50% team based and 50% department based.

Example 2: Susan has just been asked to work on a special project team that is being formed to increase sales to one of the company's biggest customers. Because this is a significant assignment, she'll spend about 70% of her time on that team. She'll spend the other 30% of her time in the Engineering Department that originally hired her, on tasks planned by that department's newly formed team. Susan's time is divided 70% with the Sales Project Team and 30% with the Engineering Department Team.

As team leader you will need to help members understand that:

• No two members will have the same work profile,

• Some people will work on one team for 100% of their time, while others will work on a number of teams,

• Some people will work on a team and also in a functional department,

• The proportion of time people spend on various teams and assignments might change as team work loads ebb and flow.

How Being on a Team Changes Work Habits

On a daily basis there are some real differences in how team members conduct themselves, as compared to the members of a functional department.

The following chart outlines some of the key differences.

Before teams:		On a team:
Go to a supervisor for big decisions	⟶	Make decisions with teammates
Get work assigned	⟶	Create work plans with teammates
Get evaluated	⟶	Set targets and monitor own results
Attend few meetings	⟶	Attend regular team meetings
Engage in little training	⟶	Much more learning of new skills
Do my work alone	⟶	Continue to do most work alone

Understanding Team Development

All team leaders need to understand that teams go through stages in their development that make them behave differently at different times. These stages of team growth are: forming, storming, norming, and performing.

Because you're going to be leading a new team, you need to pay particular attention to the traits of the forming stage.

Stage 1 - Forming

In the "forming" stage, team members usually feel some excitement and eagerness at the promise of a new enterprise. It's not unusual for expectations to be quite high. In spite of this, new members also experience anxiety about where they fit in and what's expected of them. They're wondering: *"Do I have the right skills? Will people like me? Will I like them? Can we achieve our goal?"*

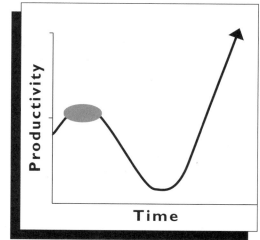

In reaction to this anxiety, it's common for most new members to sit back quietly until they've sized up the situation. A rare few may respond to the situation by challenging the scope of the assignment, other members of the group, or the leader.

Most new team members will express their uncertainty about what is ahead by being quite dependent on you, the leader, to give them a sense of place and structure. The main concerns of most new members is finding a "position" for themselves on the team.

Handling a Team in Forming

The best strategy for a team leader at this stage is to recognize that people want and need the comfort of structure. Your greatest contribution will be to provide orientation, create a clear framework within which the team can operate, set a comfortable climate, help members define their goals, and clarify roles for team members so they are clear about what they will be doing.

The activities described in this book as part of the "Team Launch" process have been created to respond to the specific challenges of the forming stage by providing the structure a new team needs.

Stage 2 - Storming

At some point after formation, most teams will "storm." This is such a predictable stage that you can expect it to happen. We know that if the formation process has been managed properly, "storming" will probably be lighter and short-lived. On the other hand, if the team was improperly formed in the first

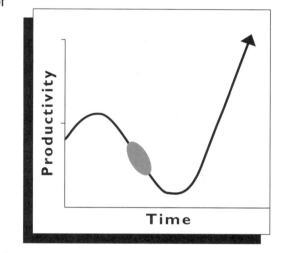

place and then poorly led, storming can go on for months and be very debilitating.

Storming takes place when members experience disappointment that their initial hopes for the team aren't realized. Instead they start running into the realities of working together. Teams can storm about the volume of work, tight time frames, or the frustration of long meetings.

Members may also storm against each other. Cliques can form or people may start rubbing others the wrong way. Power struggles are common at this stage. Because the team leader has most of the power on a new team, expect power struggles to be aimed at you. This can manifest itself as people holding meetings without inviting you, changing something you requested they do, or directly contradicting you during meetings.

Storming is the toughest stage for any new team. Following the high hopes and optimism of the forming stage, the conflicts and frustration of storming are discouraging to say the least. It's important, therefore, to understand that storming isn't the death of the team. Instead it should be viewed as an adolescent phase in which the members are expressing their concerns and spreading their wings. The turning point for you as the leader is in responding to storming with the right strategies.

Handling a Team That's Storming

Being able to handle storming is so important that we have devoted a separate volume to storming management strategies. This book is called *Advanced Team Facilitation* and is available to order from GOAL/QPC (www.goalqpc.com). Because the scope of this workbook is on the forming stage of team development, we are providing only the briefest description about storming strategies here.

The main role of the team leader during storming is to understand that the team needs to surface issues and learn to deal with conflict. The leader also has to spend time improving member skills at working together.

The biggest mistake a leader can make at the first sign of serious storming is to step in to suppress the conflict by asking people to get along, or to start solving all of their interpersonal problems in private meetings outside the team meetings. This is a mistake because it reinforces member dependence on the leader and doesn't allow the members to gain experience settling their own conflicts.

Storming requires that the team focus on interpersonal dynamics instead of achieving its goals and work plans. That's why storming is a period of reduced productivity — the team is essentially distracted from its task by having to focus on its internal problems.

Handling storming successfully demands highly developed facilitation skills on the part of the leader, who has to stay neutral while members use feedback and problem-solving techniques to surface and resolve issues.

Some of the facilitative strategies that leaders need to use to end storming include:

- Accept tension as normal,
- Stay totally calm and neutral,
- Create an atmosphere where people can safely express feelings,
- Assertively referee any heated discussions,
- Openly admit there is conflict,
- Help members identify issues,
- Invite input and feedback,
- Facilitate communication.

When members are encouraged to settle their own problems, they develop self-esteem and confidence in their ability to work through tough issues. The result is an increasing degree of openness. Team members give more feedback, share responsibility and control, and express their shared experiences.

Stage 3 - Norming

When a team gets engaged in identifying and solving its problems, it enters the next stage of its development. Stage three or "norming" is a transitionary phase in which members experience an increasing level of satisfaction because they are resolving their conflicts and have solved major problems. As animosities disappear, harmony, trust, support, and respect increase.

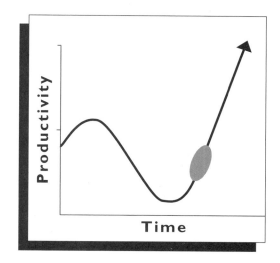

This phase is called norming because the members end their conflicts by deciding on new rules or norms for the future. Norming sets the stage for the final phase of team development, which is "performing."

Some of the activities that leaders need to undertake in norming include:

• Helping members understand the nature of the team's problem,
• Creating the right climate to help members face issues together,
• Making the right intervention to resolve team issues,
• Helping members gain new skills,
• Supporting members while they make improvements,
• Sharing power and encouraging empowerment,
• Encouraging others to assume leadership roles.

Handling a Team in Norming

The team leader's role in this stage of development is to facilitate team members as they discuss the team's problems and then implement solutions. Besides being a period of resolution, norming is also a time for skill development, redefining the role of the team, refocusing on increasing team productivity, and generally getting back on track.

Most leaders notice that they naturally tend to relinquish more control to members at this time. This is a constructive and necessary strategy if members are to emerge from the storming/norming phase and reach their potential as a high performance team.

Stage 4 - Performing

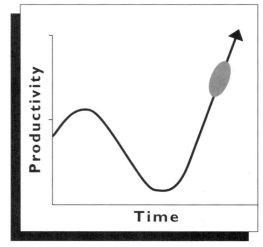

A team reaches "performing" after it has resolved its conflicts and members have become more experienced at working together. At this stage, members are ready to settle down to do the important work of the organization. The distractions of the storming phase are now behind the team and members feel that real progress is being made. As a result there is typically a feeling of excitement about participating in team activities and working collaboratively.

In the performing stage, members know each other's skills and are now working interdependently. There is a feeling of team strength and members typically exhibit high confidence in their ability to accomplish tasks and share the leadership role. A team in performing usually knows it has reached a higher level of productivity.

Handling a Team That's Performing

While leading a team that's reached high performance is much easier than handling a team in the earlier stages, it has its own challenges. The leader has to be very careful not to take back control or dominate. The members are now taking charge and the relationship needs to resemble that of a parent and a grown child. There needs to be mutual respect and more letting go of power. A kind of collegiality between the leader and the members often emerges. In fact, if the leader has done a good job of building the team, he or she should be able to stop being the leader all of the time. In a high performance team, leadership and facilitation duties are shared to such an extent that the leader is freed up to act more like a member and offer technical expertise to the group.

....

As a new team leader you need to know that your team will go through all of these developmental stages. In fact, it might go through some of them several times. For example:

If the team loses a significant number of members at the same time, the team will automatically revert to the forming stage for at least a few meetings, until new members are integrated into the team. Teams can also storm several times, over different issues.

While no developmental stage is bad and each is a part of the journey, you need to be clear that the goal of all team leaders should be to help the team reach *high performance* as quickly as possible. It shouldn't be your goal to create teams that either stay in the dependent forming stage forever, or thrash around for months in the storming phase.

People often ask whether it's mandatory to go through the storming stage. Unfortunately, storming is a normal part of growing to maturity. We all know that some teens are rebellious for years while others get through adolescence more smoothly. Regardless of how intense it is, all teams have to go through some sort of period of testing and learning.

The goal of team leaders isn't to skip storming, but to understand that it's coming, learn strategies to get through it, and get to the high performance stage as quickly as possible.

The other key thing that will reduce the severity of storming is to lay a proper foundation for your team. If the team gets off on the right foot with clear goals, rules, and plans, they are less likely to storm as intensely. A sound Team Launch is, therefore, the first strategy for getting to "performing" fast.

Getting Clear about Empowerment

At the heart of the shift from the traditional command-and-control management model to a team-based culture is the concept of empowerment. Without empowerment there can be no delegation, no teams, and no close-to-the-customer responses.

During the past decade, thousands of innovative and responsive organizations have learned about the importance of shifting decision making to the lowest possible level in the organization. But that shift can't and shouldn't happen suddenly. Anyone who has been in an organization that has suddenly empowered people who weren't prepared for that power knows very well that empowerment isn't an overnight thing.

Empowerment is also often poorly understood by team members who might assume that it means they are now entitled to do whatever they think is right.

Years of trial and error with empowerment has taught us that sharing authority and responsibility should be done slowly, activity by activity. We have also learned that increases in empowerment have to be accompanied by training and support.

The good news for you and your team is that empowerment doesn't need to be a vague concept. There is a very concrete formula for sorting out the exact empowerment level that's most appropriate for each situation.

The Four-Level Empowerment Model

When making decisions, there are four distinct empowerment choices. These four choices, or empowerment levels, are each appropriate in different situations.

Level I Empowerment refers to a decision style in which management makes a particular decision without consultation with employees. They then inform the employees, who are expected to comply with the decision. This is a top-down, directive decision.

Level II Empowerment means that management is making a decision, but wants to get employee input first. Employees offer their ideas, but are clear that the decision will still be made by management. Management then decides and informs employees, who are expected to comply. This is a consultative decision.

Level III Empowerment refers to any situation in which employees are told to make a decision and recommend a course of action. Before they can implement their plans, however, they need to get approval from management. This is a participative decision.

Level IV Empowerment means that employees have been given full authority to make a particular decision, create action steps, and implement changes without any further approval from management. This is a delegated decision.

The key to understanding this model is to recognize that each of the four levels has its place, depending on the developmental stage of the team and the nature of the activity.

As team leader, you need to analyze each task the team will be handling, the inherent risks, and the readiness of the members in each situation. From that assessment you will be able to determine which empowerment level is most appropriate for each activity.

The appropriate empowerment level should then be set, activity-by-activity. These empowerment levels should then be communicated to the team to avoid confusion.

Use the *Team Empowerment Chart* on the next page as a quick reference guide.

Team Empowerment Chart

Management Role			Employees' Role
I **Directive**	**II** **Consultative**	**III** **Participative**	**IV** **Delegative**
Who decides: Management decides, then informs employees	Management decides after consulting employees	Employees recommend and act after receiving approval	Employees decide and act (have pre-approval)
Appropriate if: Information is sensitive, team lacks skill or experience, or accountability can't be shared	Management has information and can't share accountability, but wishes input and ideas from employees	Employee ideas and active participation are desired, but risk is high or employees still lack experience to go it alone	Employees have needed skills and can assume full accountability for outcomes
Effect: Management control and accountability	Management benefits from staff ideas	Employees take initiative and implement outcomes	Employees take responsibility
Dependency: Employees are dependent	Employees are more involved	Employees and leaders are interdependent	Employees are independent
Most Effective Distribution			
5%	10%	25%	60%

How Empowered Do Teams Really Need to Be?

Teams can be created at low, medium, or high autonomy levels. There are some highly controlling cultures where teams are not allowed to make decisions above level III. These teams have to seek final approval before they spend money or implement changes.

While this arrangement may sound good to those managers who are reluctant to share power with employees, it negates the true potential of teams.

If every team decision has to be referred to management for approval, the entire team process will move at a snail's pace and a bottleneck will form at the top of the organization. This is not to mention the fact that members will feel powerless and frustrated.

Because the main rationale for forming teams is to make the organization more innovative and able to respond quickly to customer needs, this low empowerment approach won't yield the kind of results that justify all the effort that it takes to form a successful team. Everyone who is involved with teams has to realize, therefore, that the ultimate goal is to shift as many decisions as possible to empowerment level IV. This doesn't mean that the team's leader will be empowered to level IV — rather, that the team's <u>members</u> will be empowered to that extent.

Once empowerment issues have been resolved, the stage is set for teams to mature through the four stages of development to high performance. If the team is properly launched, well trained, and skillfully led, at the end of six to nine months they should be able to handle the following empowerment mix:

> • At least 60% of decisions will be totally delegated (level IV),
>
> • A further 25% will require approval of recommendations (level III),
>
> • 10% will be made by management consulting (level II),
>
> • A final 5% will remain directive (level I).

Q. Think about the decision-making style of your most recent job. What percentages would you put beside each of the four levels to describe your current empowerment situation?

	Level I	**Level II**	**Level III**	**Level IV**
%				

The Impact of Not Empowering

If teams are formed but not given enough empowerment, the organization will experience the following lost opportunities:

- Diminished returns for the effort put into teaming,

- Inability to achieve more innovative and radical ideas,

- Unmet expectations of employees who want autonomy,

- Growing cynicism about teamwork,

- Teams "running out of steam,"

- Major blocks to team initiatives,

- Complacency about change.

There are hundreds of organizations that have tried to implement teams at very low autonomy levels. They hoped to gain the benefits of team synergy and productivity improvement, without changing the culture or the structure of the organization. The only thing they succeeded in doing was wasting a tremendous amount of time and energy.

When it comes to empowerment, here are the *rules of the game:*

- Recognize that you must empower, or forget the whole thing,

- Don't interpret empowerment as simply delegating; make slow but steady progress by empowering activity-by-activity and moving level-by-level up the empowerment chart,

- Provide training and support to team members as they take on increased responsibility for jobs that may be new to them,

- Be prepared to temporarily reduce empowerment levels if the team is unwilling or unable to manage specific activities,

- Provide adequate organizational support, and work to remove barriers to team decisions,

- Be prepared to pay people more for their increased efforts, and reward them when they achieve outstanding results in one of their areas of full responsibility.

Conditions for Empowerment

Any plan to empower people needs planning and the creation of key conditions that favor true empowerment. These include:

✔ Communicating more effectively and more openly so that team members have the information they need to make decisions,

✔ Appropriate and timely training so that team members can confidently take on additional responsibilities,

✔ Anticipating problems and building in the necessary tolerances for mistakes,

✔ Having a clear set of measures for the expected results of each initiative,

✔ Monitoring progress and offering timely feedback on performance,

✔ Ongoing coaching and support from the team leader,

✔ A regular review of empowerment levels to make adjustments and ensure that there is a consistent movement to higher levels for most activities.

Successful empowerment also means selecting and matching the right level of empowerment to activities that each person or the team are ready to handle. Even a new team in forming can handle the first four or five "low risk" activities outlined on the following chart. By the time it reaches performing, the team should be empowered to make level IV decisions on the remaining items.

Empowerment Task Progression

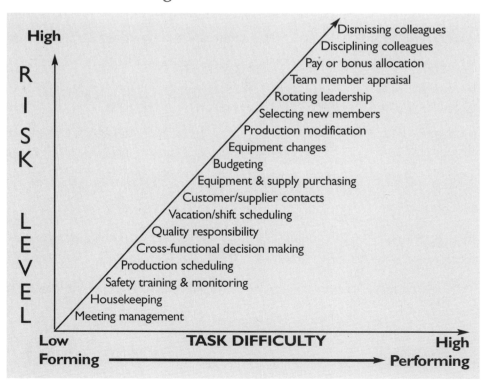

$Q.$ Which of the responsibilities on the preceding *Empowerment Task Progression Chart* do you anticipate your new team will be handling? Using a different colored pen, indicate which empowerment levels you expect will make sense for these activities after three months.

Responsibility/Task	Check off corresponding level of empowerment:			
	Level I	Level II	Level III	Level IV

Fostering Empowerment by Negotiating Fault Tolerance

Anyone who intends to empower others needs to understand that mistakes will inevitably be made. As a new team leader you need to think about the conditions under which the organization is ready to tolerate mistakes.

It is quite common for employees to be eager to take on more authority than they are really ready for. In these situations, you should discuss the risks with those team members. You need to make sure that they look at the situation and understand the consequences that are tolerable to the organization.

The process of examining risks and negotiating the circumstances under which empowerment can be enlarged is called *negotiating fault tolerance*. This is an especially valuable tool to use when members are asking for more power than you or the organization are ready to offer.

How Fault Tolerance Works

When team members want to be empowered for a specific task that is greater than management's acceptable tolerance, your team needs to:

- Discuss the potential for error,
- Identify what can go wrong and what can be done to minimize each potential hazard,

- Explore what the acceptable tolerances are for any potential mistakes,

- Identify any training or other support mechanisms that might further limit potential mistakes,

- Set up performance indicators or other early warning signals so that you and your team can monitor the situation.

It's important to remember that mistakes are an inevitable part of learning and growing. Teams can't reach maturity without trying things and occasionally failing. The important lesson here is not to make sure mistakes never happen, but to manage and learn from them when they do happen. The follow-up strategy to any mistake is to "debrief" what went wrong, looking at all of the factors so that similar errors won't be made in the next venture. Facilitating this sort of debriefing process is an important part of each team leader's role as trainer.

Q. Can you anticipate any particular activity that your new team might want to have more autonomy over than management is likely to be comfortable with?

_____

_____

_____

_____

_____

_____

If you find yourself needing to negotiate the terms of empowerment, the *Fault Tolerance Worksheet* on the next page should prove to be helpful.

Fault Tolerance Worksheet

Before empowering employees to undertake new and potentially risky activities, leaders are well advised to discuss the potential for problems. The following aspects of the assignment should be discussed:

Task or activity being undertaken:

_____

Level of empowerment set for this task: _____ Level members want: _____

What could go wrong? With what consequences?

_____

Who is likely to be affected? What might their reaction be?

_____

What can be done to minimize any negative impacts?

_____

What training or other support might minimize the risks?

_____

What monitoring and report mechanism can be set up to track the activity as it unfolds?

_____

Other considerations?

Motivating Employees in an Empowering Workplace

Motivating employees is very different in an empowering workplace than it is in a hierarchical and bureaucratic one.

Remember:

✓ Empowerment involves increasing people's accountability,

✓ Empowerment demands greater initiative from employees,

✓ Many employees are not comfortable with taking on unfamiliar tasks,

✓ Many employees resist any activity that feels risky,

✓ Increased responsibility creates stress.

You can reduce this natural stress by offering needed training, being there as coach and counselor, helping members learn from their experiences, and generally acting as a cheering section for successes!

Handling Resistance to Empowerment

If employees say *"no thank you"* when you tell them they are going to be making more decisions and be held accountable for results, you have two very different tactics available:

1. You can simply order members to get on with the new tasks, *or*

2. You can work through their resistance to get their buy-in.

At first glance, tactic 1 (ordering people to accept more responsibility) sounds simpler. Unfortunately, this approach doesn't work to develop the team's sense of commitment. People are good at acting as though they are accepting responsibility, then resisting in dozens of subtle ways. All leaders have had the experience of staff saying they'll do something, then dragging their feet so that it never actually gets done.

The other problem with ordering compliance is that it reverts the team's culture back to the old autocratic approach. If you constantly order people to do things, the team will never mature past the dependent forming stage of its development.

The second tactic (helping members work through their resistance) is the more complex, but ultimately more effective approach. It involves using the following "facilitative" techniques:

1. Clearly describe what needs to be done.

2. Ask members to describe specifically what's keeping them from taking on the new challenge.

3. Ask them to identify the conditions under which they would take on increased empowerment (i.e., release from some other task, training, anticipating mistakes, commitment of support from others, coaching from you, etc.).

4. Examine the "reasonableness" of each condition and dismiss those demands that are impossible to meet (i.e., more money, more staff).

5. Commit to implementing those support mechanisms that are reasonable.

6. Help the members plan their actions.

7. Hold periodic feedback sessions to discuss how things are going and continue to eliminate remaining blocks.

8. Offer encouragement and don't forget to celebrate all successes.

Handling Resistance to Empowerment, cont'd

Because progress in team maturation to the performing stage is dependent on the team taking on more and more responsibility, your ability to overcome resistance to empowerment is clearly an important factor in your team's ultimate success.

$Q.$ Which do you think you'll encounter more often – members who will want more empowerment than planned, or members who will resist taking on more authority? What are likely to be their biggest resistance concerns?

_____

_____

_____

_____

_____

_____

_____

_____

_____

_____

_____

_____

The Challenge of Team Leadership

Many people who become team leaders under-estimate how major a shift they'll need to make in their personal leadership style. This is especially true of those people who have been accustomed to controlling most situations and "calling the shots."

While you may have been able to control and direct the work of staff in the past, as team leader your challenge will be to get them to take the lead. To do this you'll need to shift your approach away from being directive, towards being facilitative. Instead of trying to be the leader everyone depends on, the goal of an effective team leader is to turn each member of the team into a leader.

Let's take a quick look at old, current, and future leadership styles.

Old Style Supervisors

This is the classic 1950s "boss" who ruled with a firm hand:

✔ Authoritarian/disciplinarian,

✔ Not necessarily on a first name basis with staff,

✔ Employee's role is "to do as told,"

✔ Management does the thinking,

✔ Everyone works for the "boss,"

✔ Not attuned to giving feedback,

✔ Didn't coach,

✔ Controlled information,

✔ Top-down communication,

✔ Always had the final say,

✔ Appraised the staff,

✔ People skills not critical,

✔ Had all the answers,

✔ Had privileges,

✔ Task oriented,

✔ Controlled work assignments,

✔ Fulfilled the expectations of their managers,

✔ Few meetings,

✔ Worked with people individually,

✔ Held accountable for decisions.

Today's Supervisors and Managers

Today's supervisors and managers have more formal education and have made significant changes as compared to how supervisors operated a few decades ago. They are:

✔ More skilled with people,

✔ More caring,

✔ More open and friendly,

✔ Quality conscious,

✔ Receptive to new ideas,

✔ Two-way communicators,

✔ Relaxed,

✔ More participative,

✔ Planning oriented,

Continued on next page

✔ Delegate more,   ✔ Allow staff independence,

✔ Customer focused,   ✔ Still feel accountable.

Tomorrow's Team Leaders

Anyone hoping to succeed as a team leader has to go far beyond the leadership style and skills of present day managers and supervisors. The main shift is away from focusing on financial control to supporting people. To be truly successful, a team leader must:

✔ Possess highly developed interpersonal skills,

✔ Act as a facilitator who helps people achieve their goals,

✔ Be attentive to meeting customer needs,

✔ Have an orientation to continuous improvement,

✔ Be a good communicator who shares information,

✔ Empathize, teach, and train,

✔ Listen well,

✔ Openly give and receive feedback,

✔ Get appraised by staff,

✔ Encourage others to solve problems and plan,

✔ Understand how to develop and motivate teams,

✔ Be oriented toward sharing power and control,

✔ Act like a coach to individuals and to the team,

✔ Share leadership with others,

✔ Hold no status or special rank,

✔ Pitch in when needed,

✔ Act like a model of what's expected,

✔ Understand and constantly manage change.

Summary of The Role Change

Here's a snapshot of the changes you're being asked to make:

✘ From...	✓ To...
✘ Direct and oversee	✓ Develop and coach
✘ Drive and push	✓ Encourage and motivate
✘ Authority	✓ Empowerment
✘ Manage one-on-one	✓ Manage group dynamics
✘ Technical skills	✓ People skills
✘ Employees work for me	✓ The team is my customer
✘ Emphasize the individual	✓ Emphasize the team

$Q.$ What sort of leader are you currently? What will be your biggest personal change challenge?

_____

_____

_____

_____

_____

_____

Why the Old Style Won't Work with Teams

In case you needed further convincing to shift your personal leadership style, let's explore the impact of the old, controlling style of leader.

The command-and-control management model that has been operating in most North American organizations for centuries is also known as the "heroic" model. That's because the manager is the one who sets directions, answers questions, makes the tough decisions, and shoulders most of the responsibility – in short, acts like a hero.

Here are some of the things we believed in the *past* about effective, heroic leaders:

- Managers should know at all times what is going on in their department,

- Managers should always have more technical expertise than any of their subordinates,

- It's the manager's responsibility to solve problems when they arise,

- The manager is the one responsible if the department isn't achieving results,

- Managers should have their people "under control."

The Consequences of Heroism

Heroism is generally motivating to the manager, but has the opposite effect on staff. Here's what happens to staff when managers are "in charge":

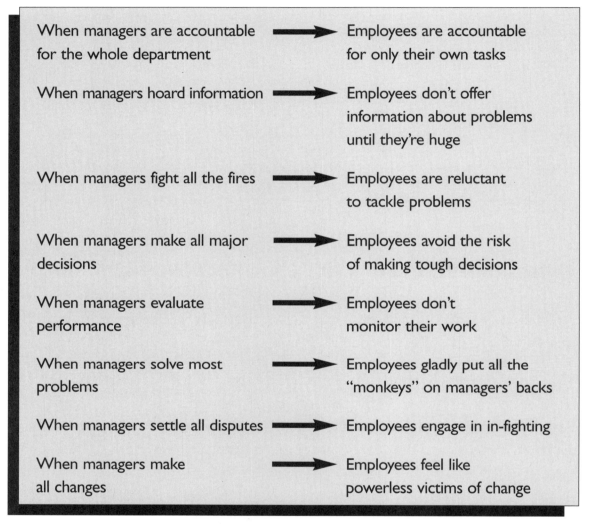

When managers are accountable for the whole department	→ Employees are accountable for only their own tasks
When managers hoard information	→ Employees don't offer information about problems until they're huge
When managers fight all the fires	→ Employees are reluctant to tackle problems
When managers make all major decisions	→ Employees avoid the risk of making tough decisions
When managers evaluate performance	→ Employees don't monitor their work
When managers solve most problems	→ Employees gladly put all the "monkeys" on managers' backs
When managers settle all disputes	→ Employees engage in in-fighting
When managers make all changes	→ Employees feel like powerless victims of change

By assuming the lion's share of responsibility for the success of their departments, managers produce the very narrowness and self-interest that they deplore in their staff. When subordinates are relegated to performing only their specialty tasks, they naturally promote their narrow self-interests, rather than the interests of the organization.

The fact that the old role models aren't working anymore isn't the fault of the individuals in those roles. Organizations have been promoting people because they met exactly the criteria that created the kind of dependency we currently see in organizations. We have also created systems of accountability and rewards that further reinforce "heroic" patterns.

$Q.$ To what extent are the managers in your organization still heroic? Describe your organization's current management beliefs. How does your organization reward heroism?

_____

_____

_____

_____

_____

_____

Today's Changing Pressures Demand a New Leadership Style

To survive in the competitive decades ahead, organizations need the kind of culture that only empowering leaders can create:

- ✔ Everyone pointing in the same direction,
- ✔ Collaboration between co-workers, customers, and suppliers,
- ✔ A lot of energy, creativity, and innovation,
- ✔ An atmosphere of continuous improvement,
- ✔ Everyone "fully engaged," using all their talents,
- ✔ Decentralized decision making,
- ✔ Problem solving at every level,
- ✔ All staff in touch with their customers,
- ✔ Information flowing freely,
- ✔ Forthright conflict management,
- ✔ Ongoing monitoring and feedback,
- ✔ An atmosphere of partnership and collaboration,
- ✔ Fast, flexible systems.

To achieve this culture, organizations large and small need to transform their management and supervisory people into leaders who can motivate employees to be proactive, creative, and empowered.

The Post-Heroic, Empowering Leader

The main difference between the old and new style leader centers around who has power and control. In the case of the heroic manager, "the buck stops here" approach to accountability says: *"I'm the boss. I'll make the final decisions. I'll let you know what will happen. I'll solve those problems. Your role is to comply."*

In contrast, the post-heroic leader believes that responsibility and control are best shared between the leader and the staff. In this case, the leader is saying: *"Let's assess the situation together and decide on the best course of action. Let's agree on who needs to do what. I will support whatever decision we reach, provided it meets critical criteria. I am confident that we will make a better decision by putting our heads together and coordinating our actions."*

The post-heroic leader is less the cause <u>of</u>, than the catalyst <u>for</u>, employee action. This person facilitates, teaches, coaches, encourages, surveys, provides feedback, coordinates, and links.

Don't Misunderstand the New Role

A common, mistaken interpretation of the leader style shift is to view it as a renunciation of all power and responsibility; a 180° swing from "controlling" to "laissez-faire."

If you act out your new role by totally letting staff make all of the decisions while you watch passively from the sidelines, you'll be making a major mistake!

The post-heroic style isn't saying that leaders are no longer responsible if their teams don't achieve results. For example, if a team lacks a goal, the leader bears major responsibility for not having ensured that members created a goal statement.

The post-heroic leader is still accountable for results. The big difference is that accountability is indirect; the leader has to ensure that the team is supported and given the tools it needs to be successful.

Beliefs of Empowering Leaders

The first step in shifting your leadership style is understanding and accepting the fundamental beliefs of team leadership. To be really effective in the job as a team leader, you have to believe that:

✔ People are the most valuable resource any company has,

✔ Human beings have unlimited potential to constantly grow, develop, and learn,

✔ People are conscientious and want to do good work,

✔ Decisions should be made by the people closest to the issue, activity, or customer,

✔ Effective groups make better decisions than individuals acting alone,

✔ Everyone is capable of making quality decisions, provided they are given information, training, and support,

✔ People tend not to resist changes they have been involved in making,

✔ People will assume more responsibility if they are respected, recognized, and rewarded,

✔ Mistakes are unavoidable and an important vehicle for learning,

✔ Ongoing feedback is needed to continuously improve.

Elements of the Team Leader Role

In your new job as team leader, you'll be playing these roles:

Direction Setter - Talking about the overall corporate vision to members and helping them to buy-in to that overall direction. Helping team members build a clear vision of the team's future that aligns the needs and interests of customers, suppliers, and employees with the corporate business goal. Making sure there are specific objectives that set out expected results.

Facilitator - Acting as a neutral party in decision-making and planning activities, thereby encouraging staff to take responsibility. Offering structured tools and techniques to the team to ensure that decisions are made in an effective and timely manner. Ensuring that all meetings make good use of time and the intelligence of the members.

Trainer - Assessing training needs, planning training, and regularly teaching members needed skills. Also creating a learning environment where people share their experiences, try new approaches, and train each other. Making sure all staff are multi-skilled so that jobs can be rotated.

Coach - Providing detailed and timely feedback on performance, along with concrete suggestions for improvement. Regularly working with each member to improve in specific areas.

Mentor - Helping each person identify their personal strengths, as well as set long-term career goals. Encouraging them to gain the skills and experience they need to achieve their goals. Creating opportunities to learn new skills. Encouraging staff to take on new responsibilities. Helping people get assignments in other parts of the organization.

Coordinator - Linking individuals and teams to each other. Bringing important information to the team. Helping the right people meet.

Sponsor - Offering support to individuals who are trying to implement action plans. Removing organizational barriers. Negotiating with senior levels on behalf of the team. Helping the team to develop strategies to overcoming barriers.

Team Builder - Understanding the stages of team development and knowing which interventions are needed at each stage. Also knowing how to adjust leadership roles as the team evolves. Comfortable stepping in when the team needs help and staying away when the team's performance level is high.

Quality Consultant - Skilled in using quality management tools to find, analyze, and solve problems. Helping the team identify areas that need improvement. Supporting the team to implement process improvement activities.

Conflict Manager - Confident and comfortable in confronting both work and interpersonal problems. Knowing the main conflict management techniques and using them well.

Motivator and Energizer - Providing encouragement and recognition so that people can achieve stretch goals. Helping people overcome personal and job barriers. Understanding what rewards people and ensuring that those rewards are in place.

Q. In which of these roles are you skilled and experienced now? Which will you need to learn more about?

Areas I'm already strong:	Areas I need to learn more:

Your New Job Description

As team leader, your primary responsibility is to build a team that quickly reaches and then stays at high performance levels.

Specific Responsibilities:

- Launch the new team,
- Assess its training needs,
- Provide clear structure for meetings,
- Facilitate meetings,
- Arrange for/provide members with training,
- Train team members to facilitate,
- Help members set a goal,
- Ensure that both teams and individuals have clear work objectives,
- Help set results indicators,
- Clarify roles and responsibilities,
- Lead continuous improvement efforts,
- Mediate conflicts,
- Communicate information,
- Liaise between teams,
- Sponsor change efforts,
- Coach and counsel members,
- Give and receive feedback.

Skills Profile

You'll need skills in four main areas:

Interpersonal skills - Proficient at listening, communicating, empathizing, counseling, supporting, coaching, managing conflict, influencing, motivating, and teaching.

Team building - Understanding of the stages of team development and the appropriate leadership style to use at each stage; expert facilitation and meeting skills; able to assess team problems, make interventions, and use feedback tools.

Quality management - Familiarity with key quality concepts; skilled in the use of quality tools such as process mapping, systematic problem solving, cause and effect analysis, customer surveys, interviews, project management, etc.; dedicated to the concepts of customer intimacy and continuous improvement.

Administration - Sufficiently experienced with work planning, budgeting, purchasing, performance measurement, vacation planning, report writing, etc.; able to teach and guide team members through the fundamentals.

Personal Attributes

Team leaders must be dedicated to supporting others, be open, honest, self-confident, flexible, articulate, communicative, empathetic, enthusiastic, people oriented, into lifelong learning, and able to successfully manage change. He or she must be a firm believer in the potential of others to achieve superior results.

Team Leader Self-Assessment

Review the following and check off those statements that fairly reflect your <u>present</u> leadership style. If any statement doesn't apply, simply leave that item blank.

1.____ I regularly involve employees in decision making on issues that affect them and their ability to perform well on the job.

2.____ I make sure that there is a steady flow of information both up and down.

3.____ I treat employees as partners and valued resources.

4.____ In meetings, I encourage all present to participate in full discussions and then arrive at consensus decisions.

5.____ I encourage employees to independently find and solve problems.

6.____ When mistakes are made, I refrain from assigning blame. I debrief the activity instead, so we can all learn.

7.____ I periodically create mechanisms so that people can safely give me feedback about my leadership. I let them know that I appreciate their openness even though I may find their observations disconcerting.

8.____ I regard conflict and disagreement as normal and necessary to a vibrant workplace. I don't suppress or ignore it.

9.____ I give recognition to those employees who do a good job.

10.____ I do not feel any less a manager when I delegate any of my authority and responsibilities, or share decision making.

11.____ I share what information I have about the organization, its policies, and plans with all employees, except for whatever higher management has labeled confidential.

12.____ When I need to get employee acceptance of a new policy or rule set by senior management, I use my participative and influencing skills.

13.____ I ensure that all employees are clear about their specific objectives and roles.

14.____ If I do have to impose a decision that is "unpopular," I ensure that employees understand the rationale behind the decision. I listen carefully to their reactions, despite that fact that I can't alter the situation.

15.____ I spend time with each person at least quarterly to give them specific feedback on their performance and to help them set goals.

Continued on next page

Self-Assessment cont'd

16.____ People come to me regularly to discuss their problems.

17.____ I know the career and learning goals of all my people, and work to get them the training and work experiences they need.

18.____ If I comment on someone's performance, I make sure that it's done in a supportive and developmental way.

19.____ I routinely evaluate our meetings and then discuss how we can improve them.

20.____ About once a month, I look over the empowerment charts for decision making and search for ways to empower people further.

21.____ I ensure that there is an up-to-date training needs assessment in place and help arrange for the needed training. I often design and run training sessions myself.

22.____ I don't necessarily "chair" every meeting. I encourage others to manage the meetings. Wherever appropriate, I play the role of facilitator at staff meetings.

23.____ I put a lot of emphasis on following through to implement any action plans we have created. There are monitoring systems in place to keep us all on track.

24.____ I am an active sponsor of staff initiatives. I go on their behalf to senior management and to other departments to run interference and remove organizational blocks.

25.____ When people come to me to answer their problems, I help them figure out what to do. I refrain from jumping in to solve the problem for them.

26. ____ I believe that planning is the best defense against constantly having to do fire fighting on crisis situations, so I work with my people to troubleshoot all of our plans.

Leadership Self-Assessment

Analysis and Planning Sheet

Look over your ratings on the self-assessment survey and make a few notes about:

1. The things that I feel I'm already doing effectively as a leader.

2. The things that I feel I need to emphasize and/or learn more about.

3. Specific actions I need to take to be an effective team leader.

Changing the Profile of Employees

Because leaders are expected to undergo a transformation in their role from the command-and-control mode to a participative coaching role, employees have to change, too.

In the old hierarchical model, managers had most of the power, while employees were cast into the dependent and subservient role of followers. The word subordinate, which is commonly used to describe employees in top-down cultures, speaks volumes about how hierarchies view their employees. The dictionary definition of subordinate is:

> <u>subordinate</u> - *adj. - of lower rank or class; dependent; subject to the control of another; junior; underling; inferior.*

While this notion of inferior beings doing what they are told to do may have worked in the world of mass production assembly lines staffed by uneducated workers, it's decidedly out of sync with the challenges of a high technology world that demands intelligence and flawless execution from an educated and committed work force.

Today we need to engage the whole person in performing whole jobs rather than job fragments. We need environments where employees can exercise their judgment and self-manage, and where they are valued as full partners.

The Old Notions About Employees

- *Technically Competent*
- *Hardworking*
- *Tidy*
- *Efficient*

The above words described the traits thought to be ideal in subordinates in the 1970s. After all, most decision were made "upstairs." Employees were expected to carry out plans made elsewhere, even if they didn't agree with them. They were also expected not to criticize – at least not openly.

Employees were also always the last to know. Really important information was often kept from them. Decisions that affected them were often shared at the last minute. Consider the employees who arrived to find their plant closing after years of losses that they knew nothing about.

All new team leaders need to be aware of these old mind-sets because the people who are about to join this new team may well be harboring these out-of-date ideas.

Here are some of the things you might hear new team members say that tell you their thinking is rooted in a "subordinate" mind frame:

"You're the leader. Why don't you make that decision?"
"I'm not paid enough to take on more responsibility."
"They'll fire me if I make a big mistake."
"Why change? That's how we've always done it."
"That's not my problem."
"That's not what I'm good at doing."
"That's not in my job description."
"Why can't I just go on doing my job?"
"I'm too busy to come to meetings."
"I don't think I have the real information about what's going on."
"No one ever asks my opinion about what ought to be done."

It's not hard to figure out that it's going to be impossible to build a high performance team if people hang onto these old self-images.

As with the leaders, these attitudes aren't the fault of individuals, but the direct result of a historical relationship between leaders and followers that is rapidly becoming obsolete.

Q. How likely is it that some of your prospective new team members will have these old, negative attitudes? What sort of "subordinate" mind-sets are you likely to encounter?

_____

_____

_____

_____

_____

_____

Employees as Partners

What we need now is a new role in which employees are full and valued partners, with all of the attendent rights and responsibilities. Consider the definition of partnership.

> _partnership_ - *noun - an ally; associate; colleague. People working together in the pursuit of a common goal. Equal roles in a shared activity. Either of the persons in a dance.*

When employees are partners:

✔ Rather than merely following the goal handed down to them, they help create their own goal,

✔ They set personal objectives that dovetail with the goals of the overall business,

✔ Partners plan and control their own daily activities,

✔ They take full responsibility for getting their jobs done to high standards they helped set,

✔ They assess progress and report on results achieved,

✔ They have access to important organizational information,

✔ They share the information that their efforts generate,

✔ Partners take the initiative to find and fix problems or improve processes,

✔ They give and receive feedback,

✔ They participate in decision making,

✔ They put personal goals below those of the team,

✔ They take major responsibility for their own training and development,

✔ They share skills and expertise with colleagues,

✔ Partners look for ways of innovating and adding to the organization's competitive edge.

The Rights of Partnership

Getting employees to shift their attitudes is one of the first challenges of every team leader. People need to be allowed to think about "what's in it for me" and buy-in to the concept. They also need to be given something in return for the increased effort that teamwork will demand. People need to know they'll be rewarded for their efforts through personal recognition and performance pay.

To help new team members gain the will to change, they need assurances that they have the rights of partners. These rights are:

✔ To be treated with consideration and respect,

✔ To be listened to and consulted, particularly on matters that have personal impact,

✔ To be told the mission and business strategies of the organization,

✔ To have access to important productivity and client information,

✔ To operate in a climate free of fear and reprisal,

✔ To both give and receive feedback about performance,

✔ To self-manage daily activities,

✔ To make improvements in processes and products,

✔ To be in direct contact with internal customers and colleagues without having to go through the leader,

✔ To receive training and development to maximize personal potential,

✔ To be creative, take risks, and try innovating new ideas,

✔ To influence others through sharing of information and personal leadership.

The Responsibilities of Partnership

The rights of partnership need to be properly balanced with the responsibilities of being more empowered, to ensure that the new relationships work for everyone.

Effective teamwork provides a better work environment for members, but it also demands that they make certain contributions.

You need to help new members understand that these responsibilities are part of being on the team. Each member is expected to:

✔ Create a set of personal goals and results indicators that mesh with the goals and targets of the organization,

✔ Demonstrate competence and commitment in achieving those personal goals,

✔ Share information, especially about problems, to eliminate unpleasant "surprises,"

✔ Work responsibly and independently without supervision, and self-manage daily activities,

✔ Carefully plan initiatives and share those plans with the leader and colleagues,

✔ Willingly take on new responsibilities and follow through on implementing commitments,

✔ Communicate continuously with leaders about initiatives to keep them informed,

✔ Freely offer to help teammates,

✔ Negotiate appropriate empowerment levels,

✔ Responsibly coordinate roles with others so that there is a fair and balanced work load for all staff,

✔ Act like a team player, placing "we" before "I,"

✔ Refrain from interpersonal "fighting," and seek solutions instead,

✔ Extend a trusting and positive attitude toward leaders and the organization,

✔ Demonstrate openness, cooperativeness, and respect to all colleagues and to the organization.

When all team members embrace the rights and responsibilities of partnership, your team will be able to move forward to high performance!

Team Meetings Are Different!

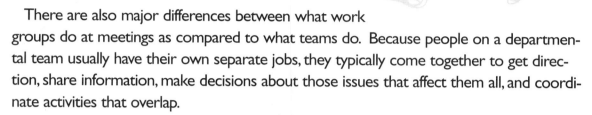

Because the dynamics of being a team only take place when all of the members are together, your team is basically only as good as its meetings! Meetings are the only place where members can build and develop their relationship as a total group. It's safe to say that if your meetings are dysfunctional, the same will probably be true of your team as well.

There are also major differences between what work groups do at meetings as compared to what teams do. Because people on a departmental team usually have their own separate jobs, they typically come together to get direction, share information, make decisions about those issues that affect them all, and coordinate activities that overlap.

Teams need to get a lot more out of meetings. They need to get to know each other, learn to be a team, formulate a common goal, identify targets, plan work, and then coordinate how they will achieve that work.

Teams are also supposed to be identifying problems and working together to find solutions and/or better ways of doing things. Meetings are their forum for making decisions and expanding empowerment levels to become more self-managing.

Finally, meetings are also a forum for feedback and evaluation. Team members are jointly responsible for reviewing their progress on achieving results, each other's performance, the leader's performance, and the performance of the team as a whole. All of this has to take place at the team's regular meetings if the team is going to be a real success.

How Work Groups Use Meetings	How Teams Use Meetings
Get direction	Build relationships and learn team skills
Make decisions	Set goals and objectives
Update each other	Plan and coordinate work
Coordinate roles	Discuss ways to expand empowerment
	Find and solve problems to continuously improve
	Work on innovations
	Give each other feedback
	Evaluate the team and the meetings to improve them
	Evaluate results achieved

This means that the days of simply getting together to read a few memos and bounce around an idea or two are gone. Team meetings have to be carefully structured and skillfully facilitated to accomplish all the things an active team needs. The responsibility for making sure that meetings are well managed is one of the most important aspects of your new job as team leader.

Meetings are so important to teams that it can safely be said that no team can exist without them. In fact, meetings need to be regular and members must attend them religiously. As team leader, it's advisable to establish a regular time for meetings and hold to that schedule even if some people are occasionally absent. Whether you choose to meet for two hours once a week or an hour every day, establish that time slot and make sure everyone honors it in their schedules.

Optimal Time Distribution

The following is a sample of how time <u>might</u> be distributed at a two-hour team meeting. This sample is purely speculative and is presented to illustrate the point made previously, that information swapping needs to be limited so that there's always time to improve the team and advance it towards its goal.

Sample Team Meeting Agenda (Two Hours)	
1. Agenda overview (5 min.)	Review and ratify agenda; make any needed amendments and adjust times as needed.
2. Updates on work in progress (50 min.)	Individuals share information on work; action items from the last meeting are brought forward for review; leader shares information.
3. Facilitated discussion (50 min.)	Problem-solve an important issue, plan future work, or make a decision.
4. Agenda building (10 min.)	Create rough agenda for the next meeting; facilitate a quick evaluation on the effectiveness of the current meeting.
5. Adjournment (5 min.)	Clarify next steps.

Your Role in Meetings

One of the major changes for you as a new team leader is that you will have to shift your personal leadership style from chairing meetings to facilitating them.

In most work groups the manager or supervisor typically plays the role of the chairperson. He or she directs the conversation, keeps track of time, takes active part in discussions, and often makes the final decision. In most work groups it's understood that the manager or supervisor has the right to make final decisions and often exercises that right.

To create a true team environment, you need to shift to the role of facilitator or take part in the discussion as a member while someone else takes a turn facilitating. While there will always be some decisions that you'll have to make as the leader, remember that teams basically operate on a democratic basis, making decisions through consensus, compromise, or some form of voting.

Let's look at the consequences of you not shifting your style. If, for example, you operate at empowerment level II (i.e., have discussions to hear member opinions, but then make the final decisions yourself), your team will never mature past the "forming" stage. Members will know that you're going to make the really important decisions, so they'll hold back and rely on you.

Because one of the main reasons for forming teams is to get the members to take responsibility and grow in their decision-making ability, you must switch to the neutral role and facilitate. This is especially important at the start of team launch. That's when members are most likely to be dependent on you. If you make all of their decisions in "forming," they'll become accustomed to you having the answers to all of their problems. It's very important to get off on the right foot and facilitate right from the first meeting.

As team leader, there's no question that you need to gain skills as a facilitator so that you can play this important new role effectively. Unfortunately it's beyond the scope of this book to teach facilitation skills, but many excellent courses and books are available to guide you. You should ask your Human Resources Department about workshops you can attend.

In keeping with the required style shift, you'll notice that the *Team Launch Meeting Agendas* in Chapter 6 of this book have all been written in such a way as to automatically cast you into the role of facilitator right from the opening discussion.

You will notice when you read these notes that you're no longer directing, but enabling others to act; not telling as much as asking. This seemingly minor shift actually represents a major change. The best way to describe this change is that it will move you from a situation that's leader-centered, to one in which the leader is supporting the members.

While it may have been possible to manage a work group with a controlling style, you simply won't be able to grow a team unless you deliberately allow members to share power and control. If you're a new team leader who has been used to a command-and-control method of operating, you need to be aware that switching to a facilitative mode may be a tough step for you. As team leader your new challenge will be to design future meetings that will enable members (not you) to do all the talking and thinking.

The Problem with Meetings

Because team meetings are so critical, it's vital that they not be a waste of time. You should be on the lookout for these classic flaws:

→ Time wasted on sharing information face-to-face when it ought to be shared in writing or by e-mail outside the meeting,

→ People coming and going throughout the meeting,

→ People showing up without the facts needed to make decisions,

→ Key people missing,

→ Inability to reach closure on difficult issues,

→ No control over time,

→ Constant sidetracking or going off topic,

→ Time squandered on unimportant issues while critical issues are handled quickly at the end of the meeting,

→ Lack of participation by some members while a few people do all the talking,

→ Ineffective arguing of personal viewpoints rather than constructive debating of important points,

→ Interpersonal hostility among members.

As team leader it's your primary responsibility to make sure that meetings are well planned and executed. The following "general" meeting principles should help you run meetings that work.

General Meeting Principles

1. Create a detailed agenda

Each meeting must have an agenda, developed well ahead of time and ratified by team members. By having the agenda in advance of the meeting, members can do their homework and make sure the needed information is on hand.

The agenda should include the following:

→ The topics to be discussed, plus a brief description of what's involved and what needs to be accomplished,

→ A time guideline for each item,

→ The name of the person(s) bringing the item forward,

→ Details of the process to be used for the each discussion.

2. Clear meeting roles

Meetings need to have members playing a number of important roles. These include:

Meeting Chairperson: This person is responsible for calling the meeting to order and moving through the agenda items. Use this role to start and end the meeting.

Facilitator(s): This is a role that you or other team members play during portions of the agenda when the team is discussing a topic and making decisions.

Minute Taker: All meetings need someone who can take clear, concise notes. This role is usually circulated so all members take a turn.

Timekeeper: All meetings need a timekeeper who is empowered to keep reminding the team about time constraints.

3. Create and use meeting norms

Any group that meets regularly needs to set clear rules for member behavior. The team members need to review these rules periodically. The rules need to be posted in the meeting room, so that members can make active use of them to control behaviors.

More information about team rules and a sample of common meeting norms are featured on pages 76 – 77 of this manual.

4. Evaluate meetings periodically

Conduct a review of the effectiveness of your team meetings on a regular basis. One suggestion is to take fifteen minutes at the end of each meeting to ask:

> *"What went well at today's meeting?"*
> *"What didn't go so well today?"*
> *"What can we do to improve our next meeting?"*

Suggestions for improvement need to be recorded and brought forward for implementation at the start of the next meeting.

Another simple technique for a meeting review is to use what is known as an "exit survey" at the end of a meeting. This consists of posing three to five questions about the meeting on a flipchart sheet and asking members to rate each element as they leave the room. A sample exit survey is provided on page 60. The survey results are posted at the start of the next meeting, and members brainstorm ideas to improve any elements that received poor ratings.

Between Meetings

To make sure effective meetings happen, there are a lot of jobs that have to be done during the time between meetings. These include:

→ Circulating the minutes,
→ Designing the next agenda in detail, paying special attention to which processes will be used to structure discussions,
→ Ensuring members do their homework so they're fully prepared to participate actively.

You may be interested to know that a professional facilitator will spend a half day designing a one-day session. So, if you're going to run a three-hour meeting, you should plan to spend at least one hour writing out detailed design notes, similar to those in Chapter 6 of this manual.

Case Study

To sharpen your skills at designing meetings that work, review the following case and try to develop an agenda that would have made this three-hour meeting more effective.

Team in Overtime

The shipping and receiving team has been holding marathon meetings lately. Instead of the scheduled two hours, they have been meeting for over three hours. The worst part is nothing much gets done! People are beginning to think the whole team thing is a huge waste of time.

Because the meetings take so long, members run in and out. At the last meeting the leader read memos and let others share information for over an hour and a half. During much of this time four of the team's ten members just sat and listened to information they had previously received from the team leader.

The team then started to discuss a major problem with suppliers, but ran out of time. This was an unstructured discussion that no one facilitated and during which several people got quite heated with each other. Unfortunately the discussion never got to a conclusion that anyone would describe as a clear consensus. The remainder of the discussion was therefore put onto the agenda for the next meeting. This frustrated a lot of people because they felt that this important problem should have been resolved that day.

Almost while people where going out the door, the decision to order new software for the automatic reorder process was more or less announced. While this was a rather contentious issue about which some team members had serious reservations, the decision to proceed was justified by announcing that time didn't permit any further discussion or delays. Because two team members had been delegated responsibility for researching software options, the other members felt reluctant to question their authority.

A few new items were quickly added onto the agenda for the next meeting and members hurried off to get back to their jobs. There was no structured discussion about how the meeting went, but people had a lot of gripes when they got back to their desks!

Case Study Analysis*

Looking at the *Team in Overtime* situation, answer the following questions:

What's wrong with the meeting just described?

What would you do to correct this situation? How would you redesign the agenda for this unfortunate meeting?

Refer to the next page for a sample redesigned agenda for this situation.

Meeting Redesign

For the Team in Overtime Case   **Time: Three hours**

Agenda Item and Time	Your Process Notes
1. Welcome; agenda overview; agenda ratification (10 min.)	Get buy-in to the agenda. Check time allocations.
2. Establish norms (15 min.)	Ask members to think back to the last meeting. Ask for suggestions of rules that will make this meeting better. Post these rules.
3. Training on decision making (25 min.)	Clarify the six decision options. Facilitate a discussion about which approach to use when.
4. Information sharing (30 min.)	Members update each other on work in progress. Leader shares new information.
5. Problem solving (60 min.)	Leader facilitates a discussion of the supplier problem using the systematic problem-solving model. Action plans are recorded.
6. Software consultation (30 min.)	Leader facilitates a discussion in which two members present software options. Staff then discuss pros and cons of each. This information is used by the two delegated members to help them make the final decision.
7. Agenda for next meeting (10 min.)	Members suggest items for the next meeting. A tentative agenda is posted.
8. Adjourn	As members exit, they pass an exit survey posted at the door and rate today's meeting. The survey results are discussed at the start of the next meeting.

Using Exit Surveys

A simple way of improving meetings is to post a flipchart sheet on the wall near the door of the meeting room and ask members to anonymously rate the effectiveness of the meeting.

Exit surveys usually feature only three to five questions. These questions should always be written to relate to the actual problems that the team is experiencing.

Here's a sample exit survey:

Sample Exit Survey

Please rate today's meeting:

1. Progress made at today's meeting

1	2	3	4	5
Poor	Fair	Satisfactory	Good	Excellent

2. Pace

1	2	3	4	5
Too slow		Just right		Too rushed

3. Participation

1	2	3	4	5
A few dominated				Everyone was heard

4. Quality of decisions made

1	2	3	4	5
Poor	Fair	Satisfactory	Good	Excellent

Before You Start

In the weeks before you actually meet with your new team for the launch meeting, it's important to do some homework. How you start this team is of critical importance, so you need to be prepared.

Here's what you need to know:

✔ *Why was the team formed? Has it been created in response to a particular need or problem?*

✔ *What is the purpose of this team and the outcomes expected by management?*

✔ *What are the critical time frames?*

✔ *What's the budget?*

✔ *What are the specific tasks of the team and associated empowerment levels?*

✔ *Who are the key stakeholders?*

✔ *With whom does the team need to be connected? What's the nature of those connections?*

✔ *What criteria went into choosing the leader and the members?*

✔ *What monitoring and reporting mechanism should be put into place?*

✔ *What blocks and/or challenges are the team likely to encounter?*

✔ *Who can the team turn to for help if problems come up?*

Key Stakeholder Interviews

It is suggested that you interview key management members to gather this data. You can use the *Team Profile Summary Sheet* on page 62 to organize this information. To build your relationship with key players, you should:

1. Meet with whomever appointed you to be team leader to get his/her perspective on the above questions.

2. Interview other key stakeholders to determine their needs and expectations of the new team. These might be important customers of the team, the leaders of other teams, or members of senior management. Determine how they want to relate to the new team. What reporting mechanisms will be used?

3. Identify and meet with other support people. This might include senior managers who might act as sponsors for team initiatives or another experienced team leader who's willing to meet with you from time to time for coaching. You should also find out who's available in Human Resources to provide coaching and training when needed.

Team Profile Summary Sheet

Why was this team formed? What's the background history?
What's the goal of the team? What specific results are expected? When?
What's the budget?
What are the specific tasks and associated empowerment levels?
Who are the key stakeholders? With whom does the team need to be connected?
What blocks and challenges are likely to exist? Who can the team turn to for help?
What reporting mechanisms should be set up?

Team Resource Log

Record the names and phone numbers of all team members, senior managers, sponsors, coaches, other team leaders, and key stakeholders.

Name	Phone	Fax	E-mail

Members

_____

_____

_____

_____

_____

_____

_____

Senior managers/sponsors/other team leaders

_____

_____

_____

_____

_____

_____

_____

_____

Continued on next page

Team Resource Log, cont'd

Name	Phone	Fax	E-mail

Stakeholders/clients/suppliers

_____

_____

_____

_____

_____

_____

HR representatives/trainers/books/workshops

_____

_____

_____

_____

_____

_____

_____

Other resources

_____

_____

_____

_____

Team Member Interviews

Before team launch, you should also meet individually with each of the new team members to build rapport and more clearly understand who they are. From each team member you'll want to gather information and build a team member profile on each person about:

✔ Their personal history (i.e., family, hobbies, etc.),

✔ Their educational background and expertise areas,

✔ Their skills (i.e., budgeting, problem solver, networker, project planner, etc.),

✔ What they consider to be their strengths and weaknesses as a member of any team,

✔ Any past experience with any sort of team,

✔ Their feelings, both pro and con, about being on this team at this time,

✔ What barriers they might personally face in being on this team (i.e., time, lack of skill, personal history with another team member, etc.),

✔ Their personal work style (i.e., highly organized, planner, spur of the moment, creative idea person) and/or their thinking style.

Use the *Team Member Profile Summary Sheet* provided on page **66** to develop a brief sketch of each member.

Remember to build a profile of yourself along the same lines as the member profile. Be prepared to share this information at the launch meeting.

> **<u>Important Note:</u>** The information that you gather about each member at the personal meetings shouldn't be shared by you at any team meeting. This information should be kept confidential. Members need to be told this at the start of your interview with them, so that they will feel comfortable about opening up.

Team Member Profile Summary Sheet

Complete one for each team member, but keep the information confidential.

Name:	Phone:	Fax:	E-mail:

Personal history, family, hobbies?

Education and expertise areas?

Other skills (administration, planning, quality, team building)?

Strengths as a team member? Weaknesses as a team member?

Past experiences on any sort of team?

Feelings about being on the team?

<u>Pros</u>	<u>Cons</u>

Personal barriers?

Personal work style?

The Ten Components of a Team Launch

Teams aren't automatically formed because someone commands them into existence. A lot of groups have been told *"Congratulations… you're a team now!"*, without ever really becoming one. That's because building a team takes time and patience, plus following a prescribed set of steps.

It is very important to understand that teams are not informal. They have a well-defined structure that needs to be discussed, agreed to, and conscientiously managed. Team building is, therefore, a complex and important job for you, the team leader.

On the following pages you'll find an outline of the important components of a proper team launch process. The ten components that provide a solid framework for any new team are:

1. Help members <u>get to know</u> each other better and create a positive climate,

2. Create a <u>team goal</u> statement that describes the mission of the team,

3. Create <u>a profile of member skills,</u>

4. Define the <u>rules</u> with which members will govern themselves,

5. Clarify the team's <u>decision-making</u> options,

6. Analyze the team's <u>customers, products, and services,</u>

7. Establish specific work <u>objectives</u> and results indicators,

8. Establish an <u>empowerment plan,</u>

9. Identify <u>roles and responsibilities,</u>

10. Create a <u>communication</u> plan for the team.

In Chapter 6, you'll find detailed meeting agendas that suggest how these ten components can be connected to create a participative and comprehensive team launch discussion.

Establishing a Team Charter

At the end of your launch discussions your team will be able to complete a summary document called *Our Team Charter*.

This document is a written profile of your team's parameters that you can use to communicate "who you are" and "what you do" to other teams and to senior management. Your completed *Team Charter* signals, both to the team members and the organization, that this team is now established, well organized, and ready to work.

When this document has been completed, it's brought forward at a team meeting for review and ratification. The final charter document is then signed by all team members. The charter template begins on page 103.

While it may take precious time to hold the team launch discussions and write up the charter, the time that your team will save later, because it has a clear foundation, is immeasurable. Without a proper launch and charter, your new team is in real danger of operating in an ad hoc manner.

On the following pages, you'll find background information about each component in the team launch process. You will also find accompanying worksheets and suggestions for activities to help make your launch workshop more effective.

When you combine these sheets with the step-by-step facilitator notes in Chapter 6, you will be equipped to lead the first meeting of your new team!

Component #1. Member Warm-Up and Introductions

Because members of a new team tend to be shy and withdrawn, it's very important to help them get to know each other. In fact you can't have a truly effective team unless there are high levels of openness and trust — a climate that will only develop if people have a chance to establish positive rapport. This business of helping people get to know each other is so important that warm-ups should play a part in every meeting while the team is in the forming stage.

Dozens of team warm-up books have been written. Your in-house trainers or Human Resource professionals will probably be able to provide you with some. If not, books are readily available by contacting the team resource publishers listed at the end of this manual. Once you have access to some warm-up materials, it's a good idea to memorize a half dozen or so and have them ready to use in your regular meetings. In addition to the exercise below, we have included six easy warm-ups on page 160.

At the initial team launch meeting, it's important that the warm-up exercise center on introductions. You can do this in a number of ways, depending on what you think will fit with the culture of the group:

1. Members can be asked to answer a set of questions about themselves and then take three to five minutes to share that information with the others.

2. Each person can be asked to choose a partner at the meeting (preferably the person on the team that they know the least). Members spend three to five minutes interviewing each other, and then introduce their partner to the rest of the team.

3. Each member can be given a whole sheet of flipchart paper that has been divided into four sections. In each section they draw a picture that describes themselves. The four pictures can be:

- Me at work,
- Me at play, doing what I love,
- My strength on any team,
- My weakness on any team.

Completed pictures are posted on the wall and each person takes a turn explaining their drawings.

Whichever approach you choose to take, the *Team Member Introduction Worksheet* (on the following page) provides a resource you may find useful in structuring the introduction session.

Team Member Introduction Worksheet

In preparation for your first team meeting, please respond to the following questions and be prepared to share that information with your fellow team members.

1. Who are you? How long have you been in this organization? What jobs have you done? What do you do now? What do you like most about your latest job or the organization?

2. What do you love to do in your spare time? What would you do with your time if you didn't have to work?

3. What skills do you bring to the team? What are your technical skills related to your area of expertise? What are your other skills (i.e., administrative, team, or interpersonal skills)?

4. What's your greatest hope for this team? What interests and challenges you about joining it?

5. What's your greatest worry or concern about this team? What could block it or get in the way of success?

(Worksheet #1)

Component #2. Team Goal

The most fundamental thing that any team needs is a clearly defined goal, created collaboratively by the members, to which they all feel a high degree of commitment.

The importance of this common goal can't be overstated. In fact, one of the things that makes a team different from all ordinary groups is that a team always has a clear, common goal as its centerpiece. The power of this goal statement is greatest when all of the members accept it as being more important to them personally than their own individual goal(s).

Here are some points you need to understand about a team goal:

- There has to be one! It's the glue that makes sure everyone is pulling in the same direction. Without a common goal the team will remain a loosely knit group.
- There has to be total acceptance or buy-in to the goal by the members, if they are going to put real energy into the team. This commitment only happens if the members, not you or the organization, create the actual goal statement.
- The goal has to exist inside clearly defined parameters and constraints so members understand what is and is not possible. This includes purpose, budget, time frame, customers, etc.
- Goal statements go stale fast, so don't laminate yours and hang it on a wall. A goal is a moving target that you have to get the team to revisit and update regularly.

A good goal statement should be large in its scope, yet give some details about the end result. Remember that the nuts and bolts details of what will be done, how, and with what results will be spelled out in the objective statements (*Component #7*) that accompany and support the goal.

Here's a sample team goal statement for a Materials Handling Team:

"To design a state-of-the-art materials handling process that eliminates production delays and reduces overall inventory, enabling Ace Industries to become the industry leader."

In the step-by-step team launch meeting outlines (which start on page 113 of this workbook), you will find suggestions about how to engage members in creating the goal statement.

To ensure that everyone participates actively in the goal statement discussion, you may find it helpful to give each member the *Team Goal Worksheet* on the following page. Hand this worksheet out during the launch session, after you have presented the team with detailed information about the parameters set for the team by the organization.

Team Goal Worksheet

Answer the following questions by yourself. Be prepared to discuss your answers with the rest of the team and reach consensus on the team's goal. Remember to base your answers on the team parameters presented by the team leader.

1. What tasks/products/services are our team's responsibility?

2. What's the unique contribution that this team can make to help ensure that the organization achieves its overall goal?

3. What must be noteworthy about our products and services?

4. How will we know we've done a good job? What should be the desired results of our combined efforts?

In summary, what's the goal of our team?

Component # 3. Team Member Skills Profile

To effectively divide up roles and responsibilities, it's really important to get a clear picture of the skills of each member.

While the leader can and should build a skills profile of each team member before the first meeting, this open exchange of information about skills is an important activity. It allows members to talk about their own skills and builds confidence and respect. It's also important that members understand each other's skills to make the most effective use of each other on various sub-teams and projects.

The simplest way to conduct this activity is to have members complete the *Skill Profile Worksheet* a few days before the session. Then let each member present their profile to the group. As leader you should resist the temptation to present this information. It will benefit both the team and the members if they do this themselves.

Because teams should encourage multi-skilling and learning, it's important not to restrict the use of members to those areas in which they already have skills. This makes the activity a good vehicle for finding out about people's career/learning goals.

Skill Profile Worksheet

Please complete the skill profile sheet and be prepared to give a three- to five-minute summary to the other members of the team.

What technical skills have you gained in your specialty area?
What administrative skills do you possess (i.e., budgeting, report writing, work scheduling, etc.)?
What quality management activities and/or tools are you familiar with (i.e., process mapping, cause and effect analysis, problem solving, process improvement, customer service, etc.)?
What skills for managing teams have you acquired (i.e., meeting management, group facilitation, leadership, conflict mediation, team building, etc.)?
What are your computer skills?
What new skills are you hoping to gain? What kinds of new learning experiences interest you?

Component #4. Team Rules

Life on a team can be either heaven or hell! If people are polite, considerate, and cooperative, teamwork is rewarding and fun. If, on the other hand, people are rude, inconsiderate, and competitive, the team will be a horrible experience for everyone involved.

To help facilitate a positive team environment, the team members need a clear set of rules or "norms" – so named because they describe the behaviors and actions that members agree will become normal for the team.

These rules or norms ensure that meetings run effectively and potential conflict is avoided by describing how people agree to act toward each other. They are an indispensable aid in controlling interpersonal dynamics between team members, because the rules have been created by the members themselves. Because members feel more committed to adhering to their own rules, poor conduct can be handled by asking people if they aren't breaking their own norms. You will also find that members start to police each other using the team rules.

Here are some things you need to know about norms:

- No two teams will ever have the same norms or rules.

- Never, ever, bring in a set of rules from outside and impose them on the team. Only the rules that the team agrees to will really work. If you have to suggest rules, get the members to discuss these and ratify them so they feel a sense of ownership for them.

- The team's rules should be posted in the meeting room anytime the members are together.

The following is a sample of common team rules. They are provided as an illustration only, so don't impose these on your team.

✔ Everyone's opinions count and should be heard.
✔ Only one conversation at a time.
✔ All information discussed is confidential.
✔ Everyone must attend all meetings.
✔ No phone calls or interruptions during meetings.
✔ Everyone will be on time to start the meeting.

✔ We will stay on track so we can finish on time.

✔ We will each take responsibility for following through on the tasks that we commit to.

✔ We will be supportive rather than judgmental of new ideas.

✔ We will listen actively.

✔ We will respect differences of opinion. Instead of arguing personal points of view, we will hear each other out.

✔ We will avoid any comments that deal with personalities.

✔ We will be open and honest – all cards will be put on the table.

✔ If we have a problem, we will surface it and resolve it.

✔ Everyone will offer their insights and resources.

✔ We will give feedback directly and openly.

The following three steps will help your group gain better alignment in how they relate to one another and perform in and outside of meetings.

Step 1: Determining Team Rules Individually

Start this activity by asking members to individually fill out the *Team Rules Worksheet* (page 79).

Step 2: Determining Team Rules

Following the completion of step 1, facilitate a discussion to collect member responses to the worksheet questions. Flipchart these responses, always attempting to link similar responses together to assist the team in seeing their "similarities" rather than their "dissimilarities."

Should there appear to be some hesitation or if the team is unable to come up with some rules or norms, stimulate further discussion by:

a) Posing additional questions, such as:

"What rules will create the kind of environment you'd most like to work in?"

"Describe how people behaved toward each other on the best team you were ever part of."

"What rules do we need to avoid personal quarrels?"

"What should we do if we get off topic and take a major sidetrack?"

b) Suggesting additional behaviors for them to think about, such as those illustrated in *Behaviors That Help/Hinder During Meetings* (page 80). Review each behavior so that members are clear about what these behaviors are.

Should the members appear concerned about confidentiality for whatever reason, have them hand in their completed *Team Rules Worksheet*. Redistribute worksheets randomly. Ask each person to read out what is written on the sheet they just received.

Make sure that all agreed-to rules are understood by everyone. Test for clarity by asking members to give concrete examples of what specific rules mean. Ask questions like:

> *"What do you mean by active listening?"*
>
> *"What would be some concrete signs or tangible behaviors that would show we're trying to do things better?"*
>
> *"What are we doing or saying that would make an outsider, observing our meetings, believe we are truly following this rule?"*

Step 3: Monitoring Our Behaviors

To reduce the possibility of future interpersonal conflict, it's a good idea to get members to reflect on their "effective" and "ineffective" interpersonal behaviors, right at the end of the first meeting. This sends a strong message to each member about what is acceptable and expected of them personally. It also reassures members that you are concerned about the climate of the team and will be working to make it positive and stress free.

To initiate this step, post the agreed-to norms identified in step 2 on a wall easily visible to all team members. Ask each person to monitor himself or herself during the rest of the launch meeting. At the end of the meeting, ask people to share how they think they did. Ask:

> *"Which of our team rules did you feel you followed well? Had problems with?"*
>
> *"Which rules helped our meeting to run effectively? Which rules did not help?"*
>
> *"Which rules, if any, have to be modified or removed? What rules do we need to add?"*

Team Rules Worksheet

Team rules represent the "rules of conduct" that this team will use to guide its interactions in and outside of meetings. These rules will describe how we want to relate to each other.

Take a few minutes to write down the behaviors you would like to see for specific aspects of our team. Avoid broad generalizations and focus on actual behaviors.

1. What behaviors should we adopt that would make us the ideal team?

2. How should we act toward each other during our meetings?

3. What courtesies and supports should we extend to one another outside of the meetings?

4. What specific steps should we take if conflict occurs in a meeting?

5. How do we make sure everyone has a say?

(Worksheet #4)

Behaviors That <u>Help</u> During Meetings	
Listening Actively	Looking at the person who is speaking; nodding; asking probing questions; recognizing what others say by repeating the point they made
Supporting	Encouraging others to develop ideas; making suggestions; giving them recognition for their ideas
Probing	Going beyond the surface comments by questioning teammates to uncover hidden information
Clarifying	Asking others for more information about what they mean; clearing up confusion
Offering Ideas	Sharing suggestions of ideas; suggesting solutions; making proposals
Including Others	Asking another member, who has been quiet, for their opinion; trying to make sure no one is left out
Summarizing	Pulling together ideas from a number of people; determining where the group is at and what has been covered
Harmonizing	Attempting to reconcile opposing points of view; linking together similar ideas; pointing out where ideas are the same
Managing Conflict	Listening to the views of others; clarifying key points made by opponents; clarifying the issue; seeking solutions
Behaviors That <u>Hinder</u> During Meetings	
Yeah Butting	Discrediting the ideas of others
Blocking	Insisting on getting one's way; not compromising; standing in the way of the team's progress
Grandstanding	Drawing attention to one's personal skills; boasting
Going Off Topic	Directing the conversation off onto other topics
Dominating	Trying to run the group; dictating; bullying
Withdrawing	Not participating; not offering help or support to others

Component #5. Decision Making

The options that are available for making decisions can be potentially confusing. You and your team need to clarify these right from the start.

If you refer to the Team Launch Agendas in Chapter 6, you will see that each of the three formats have been designed to include a mini-training session on this important topic. Making sure that members understand the various decision options early in the launch sequence will make the remainder of the launch meeting easier to facilitate.

The Six Decision-Making Options

To be really effective, your team must learn to make effective decisions. One of the biggest mistakes made by most inexperienced teams is assuming that all decisions have to be made by "voting." While voting is a fundamental technique for making decisions, there are five other decision-making approaches that can be used. Both you and your team need to understand each of the methods that are available and be clear about which one to use when.

Each of the six decision options represents a different approach. Each has pros and cons associated with it. The decision option should always be chosen carefully at the start of any decision-making discussion to be sure it's the most appropriate method for the topic that's before the team. The six options are (in reverse order of their relative value):

#6. Unanimous

Occasionally there's a solution that is favored by everyone and 100% agreement seems to happen automatically. Unanimous decisions are usually made quickly. They are relatively rare and often occur in connection with the more trivial or simple issues.

Pros - it's fast and easy; everyone is happy and it unites the team

Cons - may be too fast, so it's not for issues requiring in-depth discussion

Uses - with more trivial items and/or when discussion isn't vital

#5. One person decides

This is a decision that the team decides to refer to one person to make on behalf of the team. A common misconception among teams is that every decision needs to be made by the whole team.

In fact, a one-person decision is often a faster and more efficient way to make many team decisions. The quality of a one-person decision can be raised considerably if the designated person gets advice and input from other team members before he or she decides.

Pros - fast; accountability is clear; makes use of the expertise of members

Cons - can divide the team if the person deciding doesn't first consult with members or makes a decision that others can't live with; lacks both the buy-in and the synergy of a team decision

Uses - when the issue is unimportant or small; when there's a clear expert on the team who should make the decision; when only one person has the information needed to make the decision and can't share it; when one person is solely accountable for the outcome

#4. Compromise

This is a negotiated approach to making a decision or settling a dispute, applicable when there are two or more distinct options and members are strongly polarized (i.e., neither side is willing to accept the solution put forth by the other side). A middle position is then created that incorporates ideas from both sides. Throughout the process of negotiation, everyone wins a few of their favorite points, but also loses a few. The outcome is therefore something that no one is totally satisfied with. In compromises, no one feels they got what they originally wanted, so the emotional reaction is often: *"It's not really what I wanted, but I'm going to have to live with it."*

Pros - lots of discussion; creates a solution

Cons - forces people to negotiate; tends to be adversarial as people are pushing a favored point of view; can divide the team; everyone wins but everyone also loses

Uses - is often the only alternative when faced with a strongly polarized team or when there are two opposing solutions, neither of which are acceptable to everyone

#3. Multivoting

When your team has a long list of options to choose from, it's too cumbersome to use consensus. Multivoting is a way of rank-ordering the options, based on a set of criteria. The result is that all the choices are ranked in order of their priority, with the #1 item being the best course of action.

Pros - systematic and objective; democratic; noncompetitive; participative; everyone wins somewhat and feelings of loss are minimal; fast way of sorting out a complex set of options

Cons - often associated with limited discussion — hence, limited understanding of the options; forces choices on people that may not be satisfactory to them; sometimes the real priorities are not put on the table; people may get swayed by others if the voting is done out in the open, rather than electronically or by ballot

Uses - when there is a long list of alternatives or items from which to choose; when applying a set of criteria to a set of options to clearly identify a course of action

#2. Majority voting

Voting involves asking people to choose the option they favor, once clear choices have been identified. The option getting the most or "majority" of votes is considered the best choice. Usual methods are a show of hands or secret ballot. The quality of voting is always enhanced if there is good discussion to share ideas before the vote is taken.

Pros - fast; high quality if voting takes place after thorough analysis; creates a clear decision

Cons - can be too fast; low in quality if people vote based on their personal feelings without the benefit of each other's thoughts; creates winners and losers; can divide the team; the "show of hands" method can put pressure on people to conform

Uses - when there are two distinct options and one or the other must be chosen; when deciding on items where division of the group is acceptable; when consensus has been attempted and can't be reached

#1. Consensus

Consensus is the discussional approach that involves everyone in clearly understanding the situation or problem at hand, analyzing all of the relevant facts, and then jointly developing solutions that represent the whole team's best thinking about the optimal course of action. Consensus is characterized by a lot of listening, debate, and testing of options. Because everyone was involved in offering ideas, it results in a decision about which everyone says: *"I can live with it."*

Pros - a collaborative effort that unites the group; high involvement; systematic; objective; fact driven; builds buy-in and high commitment to the outcome

Cons - time consuming; low in quality if done without proper data collection or if members have poor interpersonal skills

Uses - when the ideas of the whole group are needed and buy-in from all members is essential; when the importance of the decision being made must be worth the time it takes

At the launch workshop, you will lead the group through an exercise that clarifies decision making. The steps in this activity are outlined in Chapter 6 of this workbook. As part of the exercise that is described, you will hand out the *Decision-Making Options Worksheet* located on the following page.

Decision-Making Options Worksheet

Discuss the six decision methods and agree when each will be used.

Decision-Making Options	Under What Conditions Will We Use Each Approach?
Consensus	
Voting/Majority Rules	
Compromise	
One Person Decides	
Unanimous	
Multivoting	

(Worksheet #5)

Component #6. Customers, Products, and Services

One of the most important aspects of the team formation process is identifying the team's customers and the products and services used by those customers. The objective of this exercise is to do a preliminary map of the team's customers and to identify where improvements and priorities ought to be made.

Remember that a major reason for the creation of most teams is to get more focused on a customer, specific product, or service. All team members need to understand that their goal as a team has to be tied to continuously improving the quality of service to the customer and/or the quality of the product.

Although the launch process in Chapter 6 outlines the steps for conducting this analysis, more detailed steps are provided here.

Customers, Products, and Services Profile

Step 1: Identify the Team's <u>External</u> Customers and Associated Products and Services

Ask the members to think about the parameters of the team. Then identify the external customers who will be using the products or services of your team. In each case, describe the customer and list the products or services used by that customer on the worksheet on page 88.

Step 2:   Assess <u>External</u> Customer Needs

Achieving "superior performance" means identifying and then systematically working on problems. It also means knowing which areas to tackle first to improve services to priority customers.

Return to the worksheet where you identified the customers, products, and services and rate each on a scale of 1 (low) to 5 (high) according to the following criteria:

Importance
How critically important is this customer, product, or service...

- to achieving the strategic business plan?

- to the bottom line?

Importance, cont'd

- to our competitive advantage?

- to becoming and staying innovative?

Need for improvement

How high is the need for improvement?

- Are there complaints from the customer?

- Are there frequent breakdowns or defects?

- Have others identified it as needing improvement?

- Are there too many bureaucratic steps and procedures?

- How long has it been since performance has been reviewed?

Doability

How difficult is it to make improvements?

- Is it within your area of control or will the change affect other areas, systems, procedures, etc?

- Will the cost of improvements likely be low or high?

- Will it be a quick change or could it take months?

- Will it involve a few people or many?

- Will there be a need for technological, structural, or procedural changes?

Step 3: Identify the Team's Internal Customers and Associated Products and Services

Every team needs to understand that those inside the organization who depend on them are also customers. If they let their internal customers down, then no one will be able to properly serve the all-important external customers.

To build a profile of your team's internal customers, repeat the exact same process (steps 1 and 2) as with your "external" customers, and record this information on the worksheet on page 89.

Step 4: After the Team Has Identified Its Customers, Products and Services, Go Back to the *Goal Statement* Created in *Component #2* (p. 73).

Ask the members if the goal statement needs to be changed in any way to reflect what has just been discussed.

Rating Scales

1. Importance to Team's Success?
1 = not very
3 = somewhat
5 = very important

2. Need for Improvement?
1 = not really
3 = somewhat
5 = extremely

3. Level of Doability (in making improvements)?
1 = not really
3 = somewhat
5 = extremely

EXTERNAL CUSTOMERS/PRODUCTS/SERVICES				
Importance...				
to achieving the strategic business plan?				
to the bottom line?				
to our competitive advantage?				
to becoming and staying innovative?				
Need for Improvement				
Are there complaints (from the customer)?				
Are there frequent service breakdowns or defects?				
Have others identified it as needing improvement?				
Are there too many bureaucratic steps and procedures?				
It has been a long time since it has been reviewed.				
Doability				
It's within our area of control and will minimally affect/change other areas, systems, procedures, etc.				
The benefits of improvements will outweigh costs.				
The change/improvement can be done quickly.				
Work-hours involved will be minimal.				
There will be minimal need for technological, structural, and/or procedural changes.				
TOTALS				

(Worksheet #6a)

				INTERNAL CUSTOMERS/PRODUCTS/SERVICES	**Rating Scales** **1. Importance to Team's Success?** 1 = not very 3 = somewhat 5 = very important **2. Need for Improvement?** 1 = not really 3 = somewhat 5 = extremely **3. Level of Doability (in making improvements)?** 1 = not really 3 = somewhat 5 = extremely	
				to achieving the strategic business plan?		*Importance...*
				to the bottom line?		
				to our competitive advantage?		
				to becoming and staying innovative?		
				Are there complaints (from the customer)?		*Need for Improvement*
				Are there frequent service breakdowns or defects?		
				Have others identified it as needing improvement?		
				Are there too many bureaucratic steps and procedures?		
				It has been a long time since it has been reviewed.		
				It's within our area of control and will minimally affect/ change other areas, systems, procedures, etc.		*Doability*
				The benefits of improvements will outweigh costs.		
				The change/improvement can be done quickly.		
				Work-hours involved will be minimal.		
				There will be minimal need for technological, structural, and/or procedural changes.		
				TOTALS		

Component #7. Specific Objectives and Results Indicators

Objectives are detailed statements that help direct the efforts of the team. Objectives describe how the team's goal will be achieved; they detail what will be done, when, with what result, and in what time frame, to help achieve the team's overall purpose. Without objectives, it would be impossible for any team to know if they're on track or not.

To be really useful, objectives need to be **<u>SMART</u>**. This means that each objective statement has to be:

Specific	- descriptive of exactly what is going to take place
Measurable	- includes a results indicator that tells us what the desired outcome looks like
Agreed upon	- has been worked on by all of the people involved so that they are committed to action
Realistic	- the targets, methods and outcomes planned are doable, given the team's resources and skills
Time framed	- there are specific times given for the completion of the activity

An example of an objective that isn't **SMART**:

> *"To improve customer service in the shipping department."*

The same objective "**SMART**-ened" up:

> *"To exceed customer demands of our deliveries by consistently achieving a 95% on-time and a 95% error-free record for the months of January, February, and March, through training and implementation of the new computerized monitoring system by December 15."*

The above **SMART** objective clearly tells what will be done, by when, how it will be done, and how we will know if the desired results have been achieved. With clear, specific objectives, your team can begin to work toward achieving its goal in a systematic and planned way. This exercise also creates the platform for building detailed work plans and sorting out the roles and responsibilities for each team member.

Remember that each team member will eventually also have to create their own <u>personal</u> set of objectives on which they will be appraised, in addition to objectives set to achieve the team's goal. These personal objectives also have to be **SMART**.

Team Objectives Worksheet

Working together as a team, identify five to fifteen objectives that will achieve the team goal. Remember that these objectives must include specific information about what will be done, how, by when, and with what expected results.

Sample SMART Objective:
"To have 100% of team members receive one week of classroom training on the new order fulfillment program by March 31st so that the new order fulfillment system is fully operational by April 30th."

Objective #1

Objective #2

Objective #3

Objective #4

Objective #5

Objective #6

Component #8. Empowerment Planning

The importance of empowerment has already been discussed in detail in the first section of this workbook. It's very important that you share this concept with team members and explain that any activity can be done at any of the four empowerment levels. This will relieve a lot of future confusion about the meaning of the "E" word.

You need to deal with empowerment at this point in the team launch workshop because the next activity in the launch sequence is to define members' roles, responsibilities, and work plans. Neither of these activities can be carried out without clarity about how much authority members will have.

It's extremely important that all team members understand:

- There are four possible levels of empowerment,

- The empowerment level for each activity will be identified at the start of each activity,

- Everything won't be automatically elevated to level IV, especially at the start.

It should also be made clear that as a part of the overall philosophy of teams, there will be periodic increases in the empowerment levels on as many activities as possible, so that the team will ultimately operate with a high level of self-management and internal control.

There are three activities in this component on empowerment:

1. Explanation of the four-level model,

2. Review of the empowerment progression chart,

3. Discussion of which items from the progression chart should be at each of the four levels for this team at this time.

A set of handouts to use in these discussions follows, and Chapter 6 of this workbook features detailed suggestions for the group discussions that will help members explore the concept of empowerment.

The Four-Level Empowerment Model

Whenever a decision needs to be made, there are four distinct ways this can be done. These four choices, or empowerment levels, are each appropriate depending on the situation.

Level I - Management/leaders make decisions without consultation with employees. They then inform the employees, who are expected to comply.

Level II - Management/leaders make a decision, but get employee input first. Employees offer their ideas, but they understand that the decision will still be made by management. Management then decides and informs employees, who are expected to comply.

Level III - Team members make decisions and recommend a course of action. Before implementing their plans, employees must seek approval from management.

Level IV - Team members are given full authority to make decisions, create action steps, and implement changes without any further approvals from management.

Here are some possible discussion questions you could use to explain how the four levels manifest themselves:

- *What are some examples of decisions currently being made in this organization at each of the levels?*

- *At what levels are most decisions made now?*

- *What will happen to this team if most team decisions are made at level II? At level III? At level IV?*

- *What are the advantages and disadvantages of this team being able to make most decisions at level IV?*

- *What conditions need to exist to ensure that a decision or set of activities is ready to be moved to level IV?*

Team Empowerment Chart

			Team's Role
Management Role			

I **Directive**	II **Consultative**	III **Participative**	IV **Delegative**
Who decides: Management decides, then informs team	Management decides after consulting team	Team recommends and acts after receiving approval	Team decides and acts (has pre-approval)
Appropriate if: Information is sensitive, team lacks skill or experience, or accountability can't be shared	Management has information and can't share accountability, but wishes input and ideas from team	Team's ideas and active participation are desired, but risk is high or team still lacks experience to go it alone	Team has needed skills and can assume full accountability for outcomes
Effect: Management control and accountability	Management benefits from staff ideas	Team takes initiative and implements outcomes	Team takes responsibility
Dependency: Team is dependent	Team is more involved	Team and leaders are interdependent	Team is independent
Most Effective Distribution:			
5%	10%	25%	60%

Note: Once a team has been together for some time and established a proven track record, it needs to be able to make most (i.e., 60%) of its decisions at level IV. If this doesn't happen and the team needs to get approval for everything, then teamwork gets bogged down, innovations won't take place, and the team will be hampered in responding quickly to customer needs.

Empowerment Task Progression

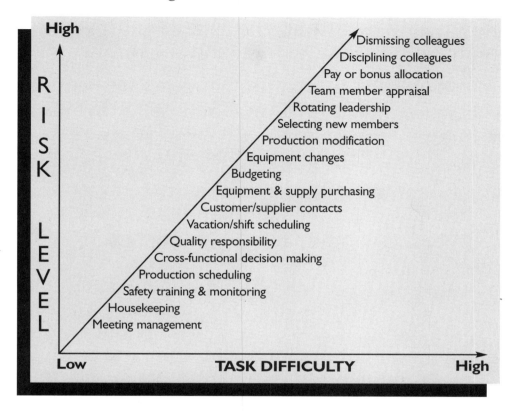

Teams not only need to have a high level of decision-making control over how they manage their objectives, they also need to take control over all facets of their internal operation. A team can't reach full maturity until its members control most of their own administrative aspects (i.e., budgeting, scheduling, hiring, and so on).

On the next page you'll find the *Empowerment Planning Worksheet.* Start with one or two items at the bottom left-hand corner of the chart on this page and create a plan to take control of those first few activities together. Make sure you specify the empowerment level you think each activity should operate at.

Remember to work on updating this list of items on a regular basis. The goal is for your team to work its way up the *Empowement Task Progression Chart* to the more difficult areas of self-management as soon as you are ready and able to do so.

Empowerment Planning Worksheet

Use this page to create a clear action plan for two to four items chosen from the preceding *Empowerment Task Progression Chart*. Choose items you know the team is ready to self-manage. For each, identify who will do what, when will it be done, and at what level of empowerment.

Example: Meeting agenda				
Activity	**What Will be Done?**	**By Whom?**	**By When?**	**Empowerment Level?**
i.e., **Create weekly agenda**	**Gather items from members**	**Sam**	**4:00 the the day before**	**IV**
I.				
2.				
3.				
4.				

(Worksheet #8)

Component #9. Identifying Roles and Responsibilities

By definition, a team is *a group of individuals who have committed themselves to achieve a common goal in a coordinated manner.* Your team has identified its goal and specific objectives. To complete the picture, they now need to create an action plan that details:

- ✔ What steps or activities should be undertaken to carry out each objective,
- ✔ Who will do what (based on skills and interests),
- ✔ By when,
- ✔ With what result,
- ✔ At what level of empowerment.

Here is an example of one such action plan:

SMART <u>objective:</u> *To have 100% of team members receive one week of classroom training on the new order fulfillment software by March 31st so that the new order fulfillment system is fully operational by April 30th.*

What Will be Done?	By Whom?	By When?	Empowerment Level?
1. Contact training company and arrange for a trainer	Beth	Feb. 15th	IV
2. Divide team into class groupings	Beth and Sam	Feb. 20th	IV
3. Prepare facilities plan and budget	John	Feb. 23rd	III
4. Send out notices	Beth	Feb. 26th	IV

Without detailed action plans, the objectives won't get implemented, no one will know who is doing what, and there'll be confusion about decision-making authority.

On the following page you will find the *Roles and Responsibilities Worksheet.* Use this sheet as a guide to create a detailed plan for each of the team's common objectives. Refer to the process notes in Chapter 6 for helpful tips on how to facilitate these discussions.

Roles and Responsibilities Worksheet

Use the following action-planning format to develop detailed action plans for each of the team's objectives. (You'll need to complete one of these sheets for each of the team's objectives.)

Write the **SMART** objective here:

What Will be Done?	By Whom?	By When?	Empowerment Level?
#1			
#2			
#3			
#4			
#5			

(Worksheet #9)

Component #10. Communication Planning

There is a real danger for teams to become overly inward-focused. Members of the same team may communicate well with each other, but don't let anyone outside the team know what's going on. In the worst case scenario, teams sometimes become so engrossed in meeting their own goal that they compete with other teams or even forget about the goal of the larger organization.

It's really important that your team have well-developed communication linkages with its external and internal customers, senior management, and other teams that may be working on related initiatives.

This important component in the team launch process consists of identifying all of the players who need to be communicated with. It also establishes the extent of the communications needed with each party and who on the team needs to take responsibility for managing each liaison.

Here are four key questions you need to have members answer during the communication planning discussion:

1. *Who do we need to keep informed about our activities? (List all internal and external stakeholders.)*

2. *How important is it that each of these parties be informed? (Rate each stakeholder as high, medium, or low.)*

3. *What does each one need to know? In what depth of detail? How will it be communicated (i.e., periodic updates, personal visits, phone calls, detailed reports, special presentations, e-mail, etc.)?*

4. *Who on the team should be the main contact person for each of our major stakeholders?*

As with the objectives, you need to make sure that there are clear action plans for each of the liaison roles. Facilitate responses to the questions outlined in the *Communications Planning Worksheet* on the following page.

Communications Planning Worksheet

Work together to identify all of the parties this team must communicate with. When the list is complete, rank them as: **high**-very important, **medium**-of medium importance, or **low**-those with whom communication is less important.

Stakeholder	Rank	Type and Frequency of Communication	Liaison Member	Empowerment Level

(Worksheet #10)

Planning for Next Steps

At the end of the launch workshop, it's important that the team leave the session clear about what needs to be done. In fact, there's a rule that applies to all meetings: *never let people leave any session without clear next steps!*

Once decisions are final, an action plan is needed so everyone knows what needs to be done, by when, by whom, and so forth. If meetings aren't brought to closure by making sure that clear next steps are in place, the whole meeting may well end up as a waste of time. Use the *Next Steps Planning Worksheet* to write up all actions that have been agreed to.

At the end of your team launch session, these specific questions ought to be answered:

> *"What are the immediate action steps we have committed to doing? Is everyone clear about which actions they are responsible for?"*
>
> *"When and where is our next meeting? Who is responsible for coordinating the details of that meeting?"*
>
> *"Which items ought to be placed on the agenda for the next session?"*
>
> *"What research or other preparation will need to take place before our next meeting?"*

Another rule of meetings is that all action plans that were committed to at one session <u>must</u> be brought forward and reported on at the start of the next session to make sure that progress is being made.

> ## <u>Two Rules to Remember:</u>
>
> - **Never let people leave any session without clear next steps.**
>
> - **Any plan is always followed up to make sure progress is being made.**

Next Steps Planning Worksheet

Before leaving this meeting, identify <u>agreed-to</u> next steps for the team.

Activity (What?)	By When?	Expected Result?	Empowerment?
1.			
2.			
3.			
4.			
5.			
6.			

Details of the next team meeting:

(Worksheet #11)

OUR TEAM CHARTER

Team Name: _____

Date of Charter: _____

Name of Team Leader: _____

```

```

Our Team Photo (optional)

Roster

Team Member	Phone	Fax	E-mail

Our Team Rules

-
-
-
-
-
-
-
-
-
-
-
-
-
-
-

Our Meetings:

Frequency:

Start Time: **Length:**

Location:

Other Facts:

Team Member Skills Profile

Team Member	Skills

Our Team Goal

Our Team's Goal Statement:

Our Team's Customers:

Internal	External

Our Team's Products:

Our Team's Services:

Our Team's Objectives

#1

#2

#3

#4

#5

#6

Our Team's Immediate Action Plans

Dates From: _____ **To:** _____

Objective	Activity	By Whom?	By When?	Empowerment Level?

<u>External</u> Customer Communication Strategy

Stakeholder	Ranking	Type and Frequency of Communication	Liaison Member

Internal Customer Communication Strategy

Stakeholder	Ranking	Type and Frequency of Communication	Liaison Member

Our Team Contract

As fellow team members, we are making a specific commitment to each other in the following areas:

- To work toward accomplishing the agreed-upon team purpose,

- To operate according to the rules set by the team,

- To follow through on personal action plans,

- To punctually and fully attend all team meetings,

- To work supportively and cooperatively with others,

- To help manage the day-to-day operations of the team,

- To learn the other jobs on the team and teach other members,

- To provide honest and specific feedback,

- To monitor and evaluate personal and team performance,

- To communicate clearly and completely.

Signed:

_____   _____

_____   _____

_____   _____

_____   _____

_____   _____

Ready, Set,.......Launch!

Now that you have interviewed all of the
key players involved with your team to get
important background information, you're
ready to bring the members together for
the team launch meeting.

This is a very important meeting so please allow
as much time as it takes to do it right. Depending on
the size of your team and the complexity of the challenges it faces, the launch session
can be managed a number of ways. For the purpose of this workbook, we are providing you with the outline of three different meeting designs. All are equally effective.
The one you choose depends on your situation. You should read them all and then
decide on the time frames and level of detail that will work for your team.

Here are the three launch options:

One-Day Team Launch

This is an intensive workshop that achieves team formation in a single day. The condensed time frame will work for your team if you have very few members (four to
five), a simple mission, and/or few complex issues to deal with. While it's best to run
this as a whole-day session for the sake of continuity, it can be broken up and run as
two half-day sessions. If you have to run it on two separate days, try to schedule the
two days as close to each other as possible.

Two-Day Team Launch

If you have a larger team (five to twelve members), a more complex mission, and/or
anticipate active discussions, you'll need to set aside two days to run the team launch
meeting. The two-day version is similar to the one-day design, but has more time
built in simply because it takes longer to hear from all of the members of a larger
team. This design can also be broken up into half-day segments.

Three-Day Team Launch

If time and budgets allow, you may decide to devote three full days to the
launch process. This is especially true if you have a large team, the team mandate is complex, and/or there are complex issues that need to be discussed in
depth. Three days is also advisable if it's important for members to build solid
relationships quickly. This three-day launch agenda is ideally suited for team
launch retreats held away from the office.

These three versions are essentially the same. In each workshop the aim is to discuss the ten key components of the team launch process and produce a *Team Charter*. Regardless of which option you choose, the same worksheets and activities are featured. The main differences are that the longer formats allow more time for discussion and contain a few additional team building and problem-solving exercises.

All of the main worksheets and handouts related to the team charter components are contained in Chapter 3. Any worksheets or handouts needed for the additional team building, evaluation, and problem-solving activities in the two- and three-day meeting versions can be found in the *Launch Tool Kit* in Chapter 7 of this manual.

Your Role at the Launch Meeting

Your job at the team launch meeting is to get the members to form themselves into a cohesive team with your help.

This is an important point. Some leaders mistakenly think that they're supposed to form the team, so they set out to tell the team what it's all about. This simply doesn't work.

> *We have learned that the only way to build a committed team is by asking the right questions so that members collectively define the details of their new team.*

That's why we have cast you into the role of facilitator throughout the team launch process. In earlier chapters of this book, we've explored the style shift required for you to be an effective team leader. It's important that you read these chapters carefully.

Because you only get one chance to start out on the right foot, here are some additional tips to help you at the launch meeting:

1. Expect members to be slightly withdrawn and unsure about the new team. At this stage they need and should get detailed information from you about the team's purpose, budget, expected results, etc. Don't be afraid to state the nonnegotiable aspects of the team's parameters. The more honest and open you are right at the start, the better your chances for building rapport and trust.

2. Play the role of facilitator during all discussions. This means that you'll be asking them for their ideas and helping them make decisions about things like the wording of the goal statement, the rules, and so on. Except when you need to state a nonnegotiable item, let them make as many of the decisions as possible. Actively resist the temptation to dictate or overly influence member thinking. The more they make decisions and decide on actions, the more likely they'll follow through. You'll also find that the journey to high performance is much shorter if you start empowering right from the start.

3. Whenever you have a good idea to contribute to the discussion, pose it as a question or a suggestion. In this way your ideas will still get on the table, while members retain the feeling that they have some say.

4. Include yourself as a member in activities like introductions and setting personal objectives. When the team is deciding on roles and responsibilities, encourage them to take as many lead roles as you think they can handle. Don't hesitate to take minor, supporting roles on initiatives yourself. Remember that the ultimate goal of a great team leader is to make leaders out of the members.

5. Use a flipchart to record all discussion points. Also make sure there are enough flipcharts available for the members to use whenever they break into small discussion groups. Flipcharts keep everyone focused and help avoid going in circles. Resist the temptation to ask someone else to write on the flipchart for you while you facilitate, even if your handwriting is poor. By doing your own facilitating and writing, you are modeling a set of skills that all members will have to learn for them to take turns facilitating later. If you make excuses about your handwriting, others will do the same. Just print in large letters and remind members that handwriting and spelling don't count.

What If Something Goes Wrong?

Any meeting has the potential to get bogged down or go off track. Here are some of the things that could go wrong at the launch meeting, along with some ideas on how to fix them.

↪ **No one says much – only a few people are willing to talk.** It's quite normal to expect people to be somewhat withdrawn at this first meeting. Your challenge is to get everyone to participate and not to rely on the one or two vocal members. Some techniques to use include:

- Start each activity with a few minutes of quiet time during which members write down a response to whatever question was asked. Then go around the table systematically and ask each person to share what they wrote.

- Let members talk as partners first, then gather up what the partners discussed.

- Divide people into subgroups of three or four and ask them to answer a question or work on a problem on their own. Then have them present their ideas.

- Give out slips of paper and let people write down their responses to a question. Ask them to toss the slips into the middle of the table. Then have each person take back as many as they threw in and read them out loud during the discussion. This helps involve the people who lack confidence in their own ideas.

↪ **The meeting goes off track – members get embroiled in an item not on the launch agenda.** This happens even to experienced teams, so you need to be on guard and not let it go on for too long.

- Before the meeting starts, hang up a sheet of paper on a side wall called a "parking lot." Stop any off-topic discussions and remind the members of the agenda for this meeting. Ask if this other item is important enough to discuss at length another time. If they feel it is, write a statement describing that item on the "parking lot" sheet. Come back to it later in the meeting if time allows, or add it to a future agenda.

↦ Members are rude or unruly – individuals exhibit inappropriate behaviors.
While most launch meetings are characterized by over-politeness, there's always a
chance that members can get into conflict.

- After you create the team rules or norms, post these in clear sight of members. At
  the first sign of trouble, stop the action and ask members if they're following their
  own rules. Ask if any new rules are needed. Add these and return to the discussion.

- If inappropriate behavior persists, stop the action and tell members exactly what
  you observed. Then ask them for a remedy. Write this down where it can be
  seen, and help them stick to what they agreed to. Avoid the temptation of scold-
  ing them or telling them what to do. Use team rules and peer pressure to resolve
  problems.

↦ The discussion is going in circles and nothing is getting resolved. This
could be happening for a complex set of reasons: lack of adequate information, use of
the wrong decision-making tool, lack of a structured approach for the discussion,
heightened emotions, etc. The key is not to let it go on and on.

- Stop the action and ask the members if they agree that they're going in circles.
  Ask them *"Why aren't we getting anywhere and what can we do about it?"*

- If the suggested remedies don't work and the discussion continues to spin, set a
  time limit for the topic, then park it for later discussion.

Final Launch Preparations

Although most materials have been provided in this manual, you'll have to do some additional preparation for this session. You'll need to:

- Arrange for an appropriate meeting room that is comfortable and private,

- Arrange for coffee or other refreshments,

- Make sure there are adequate flipcharts, markers, masking tape, screen, and overhead projector, etc., to conduct the session,

- Prepare handouts and/or overheads about the team background parameters, budgets, expected results, etc.,

- Photocopy worksheets in this book for the members or make sure that each member receives a copy of the *Team Launch! Team Member's Handbook*.

In our designs, we may have suggested an activity the team has already done or can't complete until a later meeting. Your team may not start or finish at the times we are suggesting. Or you may have a special presentation or other activity(ies) you want to add to the launch agenda.

Therefore, once you've gathered your materials and chosen a format for the session, it's always a good idea to rewrite the design in your own words. This lets you customize it to more closely suit your situation.

As long as you don't drop one of the fundamental ten launch components altogether, making up your own version of the agenda is a good idea. This will make you feel more comfortable and in control. Think of our designs as models to help you plan your own special day. The agenda you design for yourself will always be better than anything taken straight from a book.

Note: There's no need to make photocopies of separate pages if you're supplying each of your team members with the *Team Launch! Team Member's Manual*. This manual contains all the worksheets and much of the content in the *Leader's Manual*, but is modfied to the team member's perspective. To obtain copies of the *Team Launch! Team Member's Manual*, please contact GOAL/QPC at www.goalqpc.com.

The Objectives of the Launch Session

At the start of the launch session, it's important to state a clear set of objectives so that members understand the purpose of the day. As with the actual design, it's always best to create your own objectives to ensure that the day reflects your team's specific needs.

The following are suggested objectives for the one-, two-, and three-day workshops described on the following pages.

Team Launch Objectives

At this launch meeting we will lay a foundation for this team by:

- **Getting to know each other and establishing an open and trusting team environment,**

- **Identifying our common goal and objectives,**

- **Creating plans that will enable us to achieve results,**

- **Establishing rules and strategies for our operation as a team,**

- **Having some fun!**

Agenda: One-Day Team Launch

8:30	Welcome, Objectives, and Agenda Overview
8:45	Warm-Up
9:10	Introduction to Teams
9:30	Team Parameters
10:00	Break
10:15	Team Goal
11:10	Member Skills
11:30	Team Rules
11:50	Team Behaviors
12:00	Lunch
12:30	Decision Making
1:00	Customers, Products, and Services
2:00	Objective Setting
3:00	Break
3:15	Empowerment Planning
3:45	Roles and Responsibilities
4:15	Communications Planning
4:45	Next Steps Planning
5:15	Closing
5:30	Adjournment

> **Condensed one-day agenda: if you have few members (four to five), a simple mission, and a few complex issues to resolve.**

Facilitator Notes

One-Day Team Launch   **(9 Hours)**

Agenda	Process Notes
Preparation	Be the first to arrive so you can set up the room and make sure the refreshments are there. Welcome members one at a time as they arrive and introduce them to each other.
Welcome and Agenda Overview (15 min.)	Share the framework for this session using the overheads from pages 150–151.
Warm-Up (25 min.)	Have members introduce themselves as per the *Team Member Introduction Worksheet* (Worksheet #1, pg. 70). Don't forget to include yourself.
Introduction to Teams (20 min.)	Provide key points about the benefits and challenges of teams in general: how being on a team is different, and the stages of team development. Hand out any pages from the first chapter of this manual that might help make key points. Accept and answer all questions about teamwork. Use the overheads provided on pages 152–159.
Provide Parameters (30 min.)	Clearly explain the rationale behind the formation of this team: why was it formed, why certain people were chosen, what it's expected to achieve, the budget guidelines, key clients/services, special challenges, deadlines, etc. Answer all questions as best as you can.
Break (15 min.)	
Team Goal (55 min.)	Explain that a team goal is a statement of purpose jointly created by the members. Be clear that it has to stay within the parameters just described. Allow up to ten minutes for individuals to complete the *Team Goal Worksheet*

Continued on next page

One-Day Team Launch, cont'd

Agenda	Process Notes
Team Goal, cont'd	(Worksheet #2, p. 73). Then ask them to find a partner for an eight-minute chat to share their thoughts (four minutes per person). Facilitate a whole group discussion to pull together all of the ideas and record key points on a flipchart. Try to develop a one- or two-sentence goal statement. If the group can't arrive at one easily, just write up the key points for now. A team member can refine the points into a statement for approval by the whole team at the next meeting. Post the goal statement or key points on a wall.
Member's Skills (20 min.)	Have members each present their skills as per the *Skill Profile Worksheet* (Worksheet #3, p. 75). Comment on how specific member skills are going to help the team achieve its goal. Record key skills beside each member's name on a flipchart. Post this on a wall.
Team Rules (20 min.)	Introduce the importance of having a set of rules that are created by the members. Give each person five minutes to work on the *Team Rules Worksheet* (Worksheet #4, p. 79), then facilitate a discussion to create a set of rules that all members agree to govern themselves. Post these rules.
Team Behaviors (10 min.)	Review the material about *Behaviors That Help/Hinder During Meetings* (p. 80). Ask members to keep that sheet in front of them for the rest of the day to monitor their own behaviors, in addition to the posted norms.
Lunch (30 min.)	It's suggested you bring in lunch to save time and encourage members to eat together.
Decision Making (30 min.)	Talk about how important it is for this team to make truly effective decisions. Review *The Six Decision-Making Options* (pp. 81–84). Make sure each member understands the differences between each option. Then facilitate a discussion, using the *Decision-Making Options Worksheet* (Worksheet #5, p. 85), to discuss the pros and cons of each approach and to agree when each should be used.

One-Day Team Launch, cont'd

Agenda	Process Notes
Customers, Products, and Services (60 min.)	Discuss the importance of identifying the customers, products, and services of your team. Follow the discussion guide and Worksheets #6a and #6b (pp. 88 and 89) to build a profile of external and internal customers.
Objectives (60 min.)	Provide a brief overview of what SMART objectives are and share the example provided. Go back to the team goal and ask members to identify five to fifteen objectives that describe what the team needs to do together to achieve the goal.
	Work together as a whole group to identify the objectives, then divide the team into partners and give each pair time to "SMART-en up" one or two objectives. The *Teams Objectives Worksheet* (Worksheet #7, p. 91) will be useful here. When partners are finished, hold a total group discussion to share the SMART objectives and get everyone's input. It's important that everyone agrees with the final list of objectives.
Break (15 min.)	
Empowerment (30 min.)	Introduce the *Four-Level Empowerment Model* to members. If time allows, you may wish to discuss some of the questions suggested in the discussion guide. Explain that the team will be evolving over time to greater and greater empowerment levels. Use the *Empowerment Task Progression Chart* (p. 95) to explore areas of team self-management. Ask members to identify one or two items from the bottom of the chart and use the *Empowerment Planning Worksheet* (Worksheet #8, p. 96) to identify (and possibly increase) the empowerment of these items.
Roles and Responsibilities (30 min.)	Return to the SMART objectives and for each one, identify what will be done, who will do it, by when, and at what empowerment level, using the *Roles and*

Continued on next page

One-Day Team Launch, cont'd

Agenda	Process Notes
Roles and Responsibilities, cont'd	*Responsibilities Worksheet* (Worksheet #9, p. 98). Because roles need to be closely linked, you need to do this exercise as a total group. Make sure that member skills are taken into account and that work loads are balanced fairly.
Communications (30 min.)	Facilitate a discussion about who the team needs to communicate with (internally and externally), the extent of those communications, and who will liaise with each player. Use the discussion guide on page 99 and the *Communications Planning Worksheet* (Worksheet #10, p. 100) to create a detailed communication plan for the team.
Next Steps (30 min.)	Give members time to review the day, then create a team action plan of next steps. The *Next Steps Planning Worksheet* (Worksheet #11, p. 102) will help with this activity. When the plan is done, review it to make sure nothing important has been lost.
Closing (15 min.)	Go around the room and ask members to reflect on their personal behaviors during the session (as per the exercise on pp. 77–78). Add any new rules to the team norms. Also ask and record any questions that are left that need to be answered at the next meeting. Set the time for the next meeting and jot down key items for the next agenda. End with your positive comments about this inaugural session.
Adjournment	Have members complete the posted exit survey (p. 161) on their way out. Explain that the survey will be discussed at the start of the next meeting.

Agenda: Two-Day Team Launch

Day One

8:30	Welcome, Objectives, and Agenda Overview
8:45	Warm-Up
9:30	Introduction to Teams
10:00	Break
10:15	Team Parameters
10:45	Team Goal
12:30	Lunch
1:00	Member Skills
2:00	Team Rules
2:15	Team Behaviors
3:00	Break
3:15	Decision Making
4:00	Customers, Products, and Services
4:50	Closing Comments, Exit Survey
5:00	Adjournment

You may need to spend two days on team launch if you have a larger team (five to twelve), a more complex mission, or anticipate active discussions.

Continued on next page

Agenda: Two-Day Team Launch

Day Two

8:30	Welcome and Overview of Day Two Agenda
8:45	Exit Survey/Recap of Day One
9:00	Warm-Up
9:45	Objectives
10:15	Break
10:30	Objectives (cont'd)
12:00	Lunch
12:30	Empowerment Planning
1:30	Roles and Responsibilities
3:00	Break
3:15	Communications Planning
4:15	Next Steps Planning
5:00	Closing Comments
5:30	Adjournment

Facilitator Notes

Two-Day Team Launch   Day One (8.5 Hours)

Agenda	Process Notes
Preparation	Be the first to arrive so you can set up the room and make sure the refreshments are there. Welcome members one at a time as they arrive and introduce them to each other.
Welcome and Agenda Overview	Share the objectives for the session using the overheads from pages 150–151.
Warm-Up (45 min.)	Have members introduce themselves as per the *Team Member Introduction Worksheet* (Worksheet #1, p. 70). Don't forget to include yourself.
Introductions to Teams (30 min.)	Provide key points about the benefits and challenges of teams in general: how being on a team is different and the stages of team development. Hand out any pages from the first chapter of this manual that might help make key points. Use the overheads provided on pages 152–159.
Break (15 min.)	
Provide Parameters (30 min.)	Clearly explain the rationale behind the formation of this team: why was it formed, why certain people were chosen, what it's expected to achieve, the budget guidelines, key clients/services, special challenges, deadlines, etc. Answer all questions as best as you can.

Continued on next page

Two-Day Team Launch, cont'd

Agenda	Process Notes
Team Goal (45 min.)	Explain that a team goal is a statement of purpose jointly created by the members. Be clear that it has to stay within the parameters just described. Allow up to ten minutes for individuals to complete the *Team Goal Worksheet* (Worksheet #2, p. 73). Then ask them to find a partner for an eight-minute chat to share their thoughts (four minutes per person). Once the eight minutes are up, ask everyone to find a new partner and repeat the partner discussion for another eight minutes. Following this, ask everyone to find a third partner for one more round, but this time shorten their discussions to a total of four minutes (two minutes per person). At the end, have everyone return to their original seats. (<u>Note:</u> You may participate in the partner discussions if there are an uneven number of members, but take care not to dominate with your ideas.)
Team Goal Plenary (60 min.)	Next, facilitate a total group discussion to pull together ideas and record key points on a flipchart. Try to develop a one- or two-sentence goal statement. If the group can't arrive at one easily, just work with the key points for now. A team member can volunteer to work on a statement for approval by the whole team at the next meeting. Post the goal statement or the key points on a wall.
Lunch	It's suggested you bring in lunch to save time and encourage members to eat together.

Two-Day Team Launch, cont'd

Agenda	Process Notes
Member's Skills (60 min.)	Have members present their skills as per the *Skill Profile Worksheet* (Worksheet #3, p. 75). Make observations about how specific member skills are going to help the team achieve its goal. Record key skills beside each member's name on a flipchart. Post this on a wall.
Team Rules (45 min.)	Introduce the importance of having a set of rules that are created by the members. Give each person five minutes to work on the *Team Rules Worksheet* (Worksheet #4, p. 79), then facilitate a discussion to create a set of rules that all members agree to govern themselves by. Post these rules.
Team Behaviors (15 min.)	Review *Behaviors That Help/Hinder During Meetings* (p. 80). Ask members to keep that sheet in front of them for the rest of the day to monitor their own behaviors. Tell them you'll be asking each person to report the next day on what they do that both helps and hinders this session.
Break (15 min.)	
Decision Making (45 min.)	Talk about how important it is for this team to make truly effective decisions. Review *The Six Decision-Making Options* (pp. 81–84). Make sure each member understands the differences between each option. Then facilitate a discussion, using the *Decision-Making Options Worksheet* (Worksheet #5, p. 85) to discuss the pros and cons of each approach and to agree when each should be used.

Continued on next page

Two-Day Team Launch, cont'd

Agenda	Process Notes
Customers, Products, and Services (50 min.)	Discuss the importance of identifying the customers, products, and services of your team. Follow the discussion guide (pp. 86–87) and Worksheets #6a and #6b (pp. 88–89) to build a profile of external and internal customers.
Exit Survey	Post the exit survey (p. 161) on a wall near the exit. Have members answer the survey questions as they leave. Remind members of the start time of the next session. End on a positive note.
Adjournment	

Facilitator Notes

Two-Day Team Launch   Day Two (9 Hours)

Agenda	Process Notes
Welcome (15 min.)	Welcome members to Day Two and share the details of the agenda.
Exit Survey Review (15 min.)	Review the exit survey completed at the end of Day One. Ask members for their interpretation of the voting. Focus on any items that got a low rating. Ask: *"Why did that item get low ratings?"* *"What needs to be done to improve that rating?"* Discuss improvement ideas, and plan to implement as many as possible right away.
Warm-Up (45 min.)	Conduct your favorite warm-up activity. If you don't have one, you can try one of the warm-up exercises on p. 160 of the *Launch Tool Kit.*
Objectives (30 min.)	Provide a brief overview of what SMART objectives are and share the example provided. Go back and review the team goal statement. Work together to identify five to fifteen objectives that describe what the team needs to do together to achieve their goal.
Break (15 min.)	
Objectives, cont'd (40 min.)	Divide the team into subgroups of two to four members and give each subgroup one or two objectives to "SMART-en up." Ask people to choose to work on specific objectives based on their background or their interests. The *Team Objectives Worksheet* (Worksheet #7, p. 91) will be useful here.

Continued on next page

Two-Day Team Launch, cont'd

Agenda	Process Notes
Objectives Plenary (50 min.)	When the subgroups are finished, discuss all of the SMART objectives as a total group to get everyone's input. It's absolutely essential that everyone can live with the final list of objectives. Record all objectives on flipcharts.
Lunch (30 min.)	It's suggested that you have lunch brought in to save time.
Empowerment (60 min.)	Introduce the *Four-Level Empowerment Model* to members. Explain that the team will be evolving over time to greater and greater empowerment levels. Use the *Empowerment Task Progression Chart* (p. 95) to explore areas of team self-management.
	Discuss examples of how specific decisions are being made at the present time. Explore which decisions could be made at higher levels now. Ask members to identify one or two items from the bottom of the chart and use the *Empowerment Planning Worksheet* (Worksheet #8, p. 96) to describe (and possibly increase) the empowerment of these items.
	Be sure to discuss the conditions, training, and support members will need, to take on increased empowerment.
Roles and Responsibilities (90 min.)	Return to the team's SMART objectives and for each one, identify what will be done, who will do it, by when, and at what empowerment level, using the *Roles and Responsibilities Worksheet* (Worksheet #9, p. 98).
	Because roles need to be closely linked, you are advised to do this exercise as a total group. Make sure that skills are taken into account and that work loads are balanced fairly.

Two-Day Team Launch, *cont'd*

Agenda	Process Notes
Break (15 min.)	
Communications (60 min.)	Facilitate a discussion about who the team needs to communicate with (internally and externally), the extent of those communications, and who will liaise with each player. Use the *Communications Planning Worksheet* (Worksheet #10, p. 100) to create a detailed communication plan for the team.
Next Steps (45 min.)	Give members time to review the day, then create a team action plan of next steps. The *Next Steps Planning Worksheet* (Worksheet #11, p. 102) will help with this activity. When the plan is complete, review key items to make sure nothing important has been lost.
Closing (30 min.)	Go around the room and ask members to reflect on what makes them both effective and ineffective on the team. Also refer back to the posted *Team Rules*. Ask each person what they can do to enhance their personal effectiveness. Also ask members what questions about the team still need to be answered at the next meeting. Review any items that were parked during the day and include them in your planning of the next meeting's agenda. Set the time for the next meeting. End with your positive comments about this inaugural session.
Adjournment	Hand out the *Team Launch Evaluation Form* in the *Launch Tool Kit* (p. 170) and invite members to rate the last two days (anonymously). Have them hand in the evaluation form at least three days before the next meeting.

Agenda: Three-Day Team Launch

Day One

8:30	Welcome, Objectives, and Agenda Overview
8:45	Warm-Up
9:30	Introduction to Teams
10:00	Break
10:15	Team Parameters
10:45	Team Goal
12:00	Lunch
1:00	Member's Skills
2:00	Team Rules
2:45	Team Behaviors
3:00	Break
3:15	Decision Making
4:15	Closing Comments
4:30	Adjournment

> **If time and budgets allow, you may choose to devote three days to team launch. Use this agenda if your team is large, you have a complex mission, or there are issues to be resolved. Three days also allows for extra team building activities.**

Continued on next page

Agenda: Three-Day Team Launch, cont'd

Day Two

8:30	Welcome and Overview of Day Two Agenda
8:45	Exit Survey/Recap of Day One
9:00	Warm-Up
9:30	Customers, Products, and Services
10:00	Break
10:15	Customers, Products, and Services (cont'd)
11:00	Issues Identification
12:00	Lunch
1:00	Objectives
3:15	Break
3:30	Team Effectiveness Review
4:15	Closing
4:30	Adjournment

Continued on next page

Agenda: Three-Day Team Launch, cont'd

Day Three

8:30	Welcome and Overview of Day Three Agenda
8:45	Recap of Day Two
9:15	Warm-Up
10:00	Break
10:15	Empowerment Planning
11:00	Roles and Responsibilities
12:00	Lunch
1:00	Communications Planning
2:00	Next Steps Planning
3:00	Break
3:15	Peer Review
4:15	Closing
4:30	Adjournment

Facilitator Notes

Three-Day Team Launch   Day One (8 Hours)

Agenda	Process Notes
Preparation	Be the first to arrive so you can set up the room and make sure the refreshments are there. Welcome members one at a time as they arrive and introduce them to each other.
Welcome and Agenda Overview (15 min.)	Share the objectives for the session using the overheads from pages 150–151.
Warm-Up (45 min.)	Have members introduce themselves as per the *Team Member Introduction Worksheet* (Worksheet #1, p. 70). Don't forget to include yourself.
Introduction to Teams (30 min.)	Provide key points about the benefits and challenges of teams in general: how being on a team is different and the stages of team development. Hand out any pages from Chapter 1 of this manual that might help make key points. Use the overheads provided on pages 152–159.
Break (15 min.)	
Provide Parameters (30 min.)	Clearly explain the rationale behind the formation of this team: why was it formed, why certain people were chosen, what it's expected to achieve, the budget guidelines, key clients/services, special challenges, deadlines, etc. Answer all questions as best as you can.

Continued on next page

Three-Day Team Launch, cont'd

Agenda	Process Notes
Team Goal (30 min.)	Explain that a team goal is a statement of purpose jointly created by the members. Be clear that it has to stay within the parameters just described. Allow up to ten minutes for individuals to complete the *Team Goal Worksheet* (Worksheet #2, p. 73). Then ask them to find a partner for an eight-minute chat to share their thoughts (four minutes per person). Once the eight minutes are up, ask everyone to find a new partner and repeat the partner discussion again, allowing four minutes per person. Following this, have everyone find a third partner for one more round, but this time shorten their discussions to a total of four minutes (two minutes per person). At the end, have everyone return to their original seats. (*Note*: You may participate in the partner discussions if there are an uneven number of members, but take care not to dominate with your ideas.)
Team Goal Plenary (45 min.)	Next, facilitate a total group discussion to pull together all of the ideas and record key points on a flipchart. Try to develop a one- or two-sentence goal statement. If the group can't arrive at one easily, just work with the key points for now. A team member can volunteer to work on a statement for approval by the whole team at the next meeting. Post the goal statement or the key points on a wall.
Lunch (60 min.)	
Member's Skills (60 min.)	Members present their skills (best if completed before this meeting) as per the *Skill Profile Worksheet* (Worksheet #3, p. 75). Make observations about how specific member skills are going to help the team achieve its goal. Record key skills beside each member's name on a flipchart. Post this on a wall.

Three-Day Team Launch, cont'd

Agenda	Process Notes
Team Rules (45 min.)	Introduce the importance of having a set of rules that are created by the members. Give each person five minutes to work on the *Team Rules Worksheet* (Worksheet #4, p. 79), then facilitate a discussion to create a set of rules that all members agree to govern themselves by. Post these rules.
Team Behaviors (15 min.)	Review *Behaviors That Help/Hinder During Meetings* (p. 80). Ask members to keep that sheet in front of them for the rest of the day to monitor their own behaviors. Tell them you'll be asking each person to report the next day on what they do that makes them both effective and ineffective.
Break (15 min.)	
Decision Making (60 min.)	Talk about how important it is for this team to make truly effective decisions. Review *The Six Decision-Making Options* (pp. 81–84). Make sure each member understands the differences between each option. Divide the group into either three or six groups. Ask each group to look at either one or two of the decision styles. Have the groups discuss the pros and cons of each decision option and determine when that option is appropriate. Use the *Decision-Making Options Worksheet* (Worksheet #5, p. 85). Have each group report back their results and make sure that everyone is clear about when this team will make use of each decision option.

Continued on next page

Three-Day Team Launch, cont'd

Agenda	Process Notes
Closing (15 min.)	Thank members for their input and contribution during the first day. Post the exit survey from p. 161 on the wall near the exit door. Ask members to answer each question as they leave. Inform members that the survey will be discussed at the start of the next day's session.
Adjournment	

Three-Day Team Launch   Day Two (8 Hours)

Agenda	Process Notes
Welcome (15 min.)	Welcome members to Day Two and share the details of the Day Two agenda.
Exit Survey Review (15 min.)	Review the exit survey completed at the end of Day One. Ask members for their interpretation of the voting. Focus on the items that got low ratings. Ask: *"Why did that item get low ratings?"* *"What needs to be done to improve the ratings?"* Discuss improvement ideas, and plan to implement as many as possible right away.
Warm-Up (30 min.)	Conduct your favorite warm-up activity. If you don't have one, you can try one of the warm-up exercises on p. 160 of the *Launch Tool Kit.*
Customers, Products, and Services (30 min.)	Discuss the importance of identifying the customers, products, and services of your team. Follow the discussion guide (pp. 86–87) to build a profile of internal and external customers. Begin by working as a whole team to name all of the team's external and internal customers.

Three-Day Team Launch, cont'd

Agenda	Process Notes
Break (15 min.)	

Customers, Products, and Services
(45 min.)
	Once all the customers have been identified, divide the team into subgroups of two to four members. Have each subgroup take one or two customers in each category and analyze those customers using Worksheets #6a and #6b (pp. 88–89). When the subgroups are finished, reconvene to share information and ratify the assessments made by the subgroups.
	
	Help members develop a final picture of their current customer situation. Ask:
	   "Which customers are going to be a priority?"
	   "Which have the greatest need for attention from the team?"
	   "Which things are most doable?"
	Hold onto this information for the objective-setting session to come.

Issues Identification (60 min.)	Engage the members in a discussion of all the things that have been done right so far in terms of the customers, products, and services that are part of this team's mandate. When this list is complete, identify all the things that haven't been done well thus far. The *Force Field Analysis* worksheet on p. 164 of the *Launch Tool Kit* provides a useful format for you to use as you facilitate this discussion on the flipchart. Once all of the issues have been identified, prioritize them using a multivote. This involves giving each member three votes so they can identify the issues they think are most important. Allow

Continued on next page

Three-Day Team Launch, cont'd

Agenda	Process Notes
Issues Identification, cont'd	people to come up to the flipchart to vote on their top three items. Once all votes have been cast, add up the points given to each issue. Identify the top four to six issues that this team needs to address in the weeks and months ahead. Hold onto this information about priority issues for use in the objective-setting session.
Lunch (60 min.)	
Objectives (135 min.)	Provide a brief overview of what SMART objectives are and share the example provided.
	Go back to review the team goal statement and remind the members about the customers, products, and services and the priority issues for improvement that were identified in the last exercise.
	Ask members to identify five to fifteen objectives that describe what the team needs to do together to achieve its goal. At this point, just identify the objectives as a whole group.
	Divide the team into subgroups of two to four members and give each subgroup one or two objectives to "SMART-en up." Ask people to choose to work on specific objectives based on their background or their interests. The *Team Objectives Worksheet* (Worksheet #7, p. 91) will be useful here.
	When the subgroups are finished, discuss all of the SMART objectives as a total group to get everyone's input. It's absolutely essential that everyone can live with the final list of objectives.
Break (15 min.)	

Three-Day Team Launch, cont'd

Agenda	Process Notes
Team Effectiveness Review (45 min.)	Hand out the *Team Effectiveness Survey* (pp. 166–167) in the *Launch Tool Kit*. Allow about ten minutes for members to complete the survey on their own.
	Conduct the survey feedback session as described on p. 165 of the *Launch Tool Kit*. Implement all ideas for team improvement.
Closing (5 min.)	Remind members of the next day's start time.
Adjournment	

Three-Day Team Launch   Day Three (8 Hours)

Agenda	Process Notes
Welcome (15 min.)	Welcome members and share the details of the Day Three agenda.
Recap (30 min.)	Go around the group and ask each member to make any personal observations about progress made so far. There's no real need to record these, although any issues or questions should be noted.
Warm-Up (45 min.)	Conduct a warm-up to help members get to know each other better. Several warm-up ideas are featured on p. 160 of the *Launch Tool Kit*.
Break (15 min.)	
Empowerment (45 min.)	Introduce the *Four-Level Empowerment Model* to members. Explain that the team will be evolving over time to greater and greater empowerment levels. Use the *Empowerment Task Progression Chart* (p. 95) to explore areas of team self-management.

Continued on next page

Three-Day Team Launch, cont'd

Agenda	Process Notes
Empowerment, cont'd	Discuss examples of how specific decisions are being made at the present time. Explore which items could be made at higher levels now. Ask members to identify one or two items from the bottom of the chart and use the *Empowerment Planning Worksheet* (Worksheet #8, p. 96) to describe (and possibly increase) the empowerment of these items.
	Be sure to discuss the conditions, training, and support members will need, to take on increased empowerment.
Roles and Responsibilities (60 min.)	Return to the team's SMART objectives. Describe what will be done, who will do it, by when, and at what empowerment level for each item. Use the *Roles and Responsibilities Worksheet* (Worksheet #9, p. 98).
	In a large group, it will save time to divide members into subgroups around specific objectives and allow them time to work out the roles and responsibilities associated with that item.
	Because roles need to be closely linked, you'll then need to discuss and agree to the roles and responsibilities as a total group. Make sure that skills are taken into account and that work loads are balanced fairly.
Lunch (60 min.)	
Communications (60 min.)	Facilitate a large group discussion about who the team needs to communicate with, both internally and externally.
	Divide the group into subgroups to look at specific

Three-Day Team Launch, cont'd

Agenda	Process Notes
Communications, cont'd	stakeholders. These subgroups need to consider the extent of the communications, and who will liaise with each player. Use the discussion guide and the *Communications Planning Worksheet* (Worksheet #10, p. 100). Reconvene the large group to share thoughts and to collaborate to create detailed communication plans for the team.
Next Steps (60 min.)	Give members time to review the day and to create their own personal action plan of next steps that they have committed to doing. The *Next Steps Planning Worksheet* (Worksheet #11, p. 102) will help with this activity.
	When members are done, go around the group to hear key items and make sure nothing important has been lost. Remember to do a plan for yourself, as team leader.
Break (15 min.)	
Peer Review (60 min.)	Introduce the members to the importance of getting feedback from each other in order to improve. Explain that the team will be reviewing its operations on an ongoing basis.
	Refer to the detailed description of the *Peer Review Format* outlined in the *Launch Tool Kit* (p. 168) and follow the step-by-step process described there. It's very important that you include yourself in this feedback activity.
Closing (15 min.)	Review any items that were parked during the day and include them in your discussion of the team's

Continued on next page

Three-Day Team Launch, cont'd

Agenda	Process Notes
Closing, cont'd	next agenda. Set the time and location of the next meeting.
	Invite members to each make a statement about how they're feeling about the team.
	End with your positive comments about this inaugural session.
	Hand out the *Team Launch Evaluation Form* (p. 170) and invite members to rate the last three days (anonymously). Ask them to send you the evaluation sheet at least three days before the next meeting, for review purposes.
Adjournment	

Team Launch is Just the Beginning!

Now that you and your team have laid down a solid foundation, you'll need to work hard to maintain and build your team.

Some of the things that you need to do on a continuous basis include:

✔ Keep your eye on the goal and make sure that all activities are moving in the right direction,

✔ Update your team goal periodically to ensure that it hasn't gone stale,

✔ Make sure all meetings are well planned and assertively facilitated,

✔ Bring forward all action items from past meetings to ensure adequate follow-through,

✔ Surface and manage conflicts early; avoiding problems only ensures they'll multiply,

✔ Establish an assertive, continuous improvement agenda; help the members fix all of those things that aren't working as well as they should,

✔ Keep moving tasks up the empowerment chart,

✔ Build in as much training as possible; encourage people to coach and train each other,

✔ Get to know each member intimately – their strengths and aspirations – and take time to coach anyone who needs help,

✔ Remember to continue to do warm-ups and other activities that build relationships among members,

✔ Hold feedback sessions regularly to improve how the team is doing, how meetings are going, and how members are relating,

✔ Encourage everyone to check their progress against the original objectives that were set,

✔ Take the time to recognize the contributions of individuals, as well as celebrate successes as a whole team.

> **Your team is now up and running. Best wishes for total success!**

Launch Tool Kit

Contents

Team Launch Objectives

At this launch meeting, we will lay a
foundation for this team by:

- **Getting to know each other and
establishing an open and trusting
team environment,**

- **Identifying our common goals
and objectives,**

- **Creating plans that will enable
us to achieve results,**

- **Establishing rules and strategies
for our operation as a team,**

- **Having some fun!**

At the end of the launch discussions, we will
summarize what has been decided in
a document called a "Team Charter."

(overhead)

Team Charter Components

A Team Charter is a document that contains:

- The names and contact points of the members,

- A profile of member skills,

- A statement of the team's goal,

- A list of the team's internal and external customers, products, and services,

- A set of detailed objectives that describe how the team will meet its goal,

- A copy of the team's rules,

- The details of team meeting times,

- A copy of the team's initial action plans,

- An outline of the team's communications plan.

The Team Charter helps the rest of the organization understand who is on the team and what the team is all about.

(overhead)

What is a Team?

- A team is a group of four to fifteen individuals who are jointly accountable for a whole product, service, or specific customer.

- The members set their own goal, plan their own work, and carry it out in a coordinated manner.

- They also monitor and evaluate their own results.

(overhead)

Why Work as a Team?

- To create a compelling goal that we can all commit ourselves to achieving – together.

- To get focused on our customers/products/ services and continuously work to make things better.

- To take on responsibility and accountability for achieving results so that we become self-managing.

- To create a trusting environment that emphasizes cooperation and collaboration.

- To work as a real team in which members help and support one another.

- To achieve outstanding results in a *fun* atmosphere!

(overhead)

The Benefits of Teamwork

Teams have been proven to provide
specific benefits:

- They allow people from different backgrounds and with varied skills to come together to focus on a special customer, product, or process.

- They encourage continuous improvement in all aspects of their operations.

- They're more flexible than traditional departments and better able to respond to changing circumstances.

- Team members will be empowered to make decisions and take actions in a self-managing environment.

- Team members gain insight from each other and make better decisions by working together.

- They create a sense of mutual support and *esprit de corps* that helps in a stressful world.

(overhead)

The Challenges of Teamwork

Being a successful team isn't easy— it takes hard work.

Some of the barriers we will need to overcome include:

- We will have to meet often to make decisions and arrive at action plans. We must therefore commit ourselves to finding the time needed for regular meetings.

- When we solve problems and make decisions, we'll create action plans that we will add to all of our work loads. While there'll be gains from the problems we solve, we need to understand that becoming a team will initially add work to all of our schedules.

- Some people prefer to work alone and aren't used to coordinating efforts with others. This means having to learn to cooperate more and becoming more skilled at working together.

- Patience will be required in group decision making as it may be slower than if individuals made decisions on their own.

- On any team there are some people we like and others we like less. This means we all have to learn to work effectively together in spite of personal feelings.

- The rest of the organization may block team decisions from time to time. We have to become skilled at identifying these barriers and negotiating around them.

(overhead)

How Will Being on a Team be Different?

- Many decisions previously made by management will be made by team members.

- The team will be given expanded powers to make decisions and implement change.

- Team members will turn to each other for advice and leadership, rather than going to managers for answers.

- There'll be an emphasis on reducing bureaucracy and paperwork.

- There should be faster responses to customer needs.

- Everything should be open to continuous improvement.

- There'll be more flexibility in all of our jobs. People will be encouraged to multi-skill, job share, and job swap wherever possible.

- There'll be more meetings, more teaching, and more learning.

- Team members will monitor and report on their own results.

- Accountability for achieving goals will be shared.

- Pay will evolve over time from being based on positions to being based on skills and performance.

(overhead)

Characteristics of All Effective Teams

All effective teams have:

- A common goal, created by the members,

- A clear set of rules, created by the members,

- A strong focus on continuous improvement,

- A focus on solving problems and self-correcting their own internal team functioning,

- Clearly defined results targets and accountabilities,

- Specified levels of empowerment for each task,

- Control over most administrative aspects such as meetings, budgeting, and work planning,

- Highly developed interpersonal skills,

- An assertive, problem-solving approach to conflict,

- Constant attention to training to increase their members' skills,

- A team leader who shares power, coaches, and trains,

- A leader who acts more like a facilitator than a traditional boss,

- Team members who are paid for their skills and their contribution to overall productivity,

- A regularly scheduled meeting time (daily, weekly, biweekly) to provide continuity and momentum,

- An atmosphere of trust and caring for each other,

- A "can do" attitude.

(overhead)

What Exactly Do Teams Do?

A team is basically a thinking machine. Its output is better ideas! Members of a team meet together to:

✔ Set goals,	✔ Learn new skills,
✔ Establish expected results,	✔ Make decisions,
✔ Plan for action,	✔ Give and receive feedback,
✔ Coordinate member efforts,	✔ Teach each other and learn,
✔ Find and solve problems,	✔ Innovate,
✔ Share information,	✔ Evaluate results.

Teamwork doesn't mean the end of people working independently. The actual work of the team is carried out by individuals or subgroups of the team. Teamwork changes mostly where direction and ideas come from and how people interact.

(overhead)

How Being on a Team Changes Work Routines

Before Teams	On a Team
• Go to a supervisor for big decisions,	• Make decisions with teammates,
• Get work assigned,	• Create work plans with teammates,
• Get evaluated,	• Set targets and monitor own results,
• Attend few meetings,	• Attend regular team meetings,
• Engage in little training,	• Learn other jobs and take regular courses,
• Do my work alone.	• Still do most jobs alone.

(overhead)

Warm-Up Exercises

It's very important that members have every opportunity to get to know each other and build relationships with each other. Plan to run a team warm-up at every meeting, especially when the team is new.

The following are some easy, yet effective exercises:

1. Life chart

Ask each person to find a blank piece of paper and draw the chart below. Then allow a few minutes as each person draws their personal life chart. Go around the group and have each person explain the high and low points of their life chart.

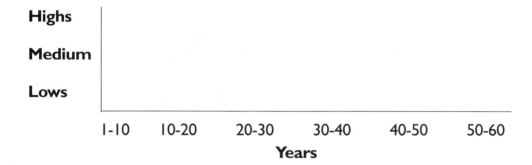

2. Pocket or purse

Ask each person to take any object from their pocket, purse, or briefcase and explain what it says about them.

3. Self-portraits

Give out blank paper and have colored markers available. Ask people to divide their page into sections and have them draw one image per section. You can ask them to draw any of the following:

• *Me at work,*	• *Me if I had $10 million,*
• *Me at play,*	• *The best thing about me in a group,*
• *Me on my last vacation,*	• *The worst thing about me in a group.*

Let others guess what the pictures mean as you go around and share them with the whole group.

4. "I am"

Everyone gets a blank sheet of paper and is asked to write six statements about who they are. Example: *"I am Sally Forth – a mother, an engineer, a pianist, a skier, a chocoholic, a Native American."*

Exit Surveys

End of Day One, Team Launch

At the end of Day One of the team launch workshop, copy the survey below onto a flipchart sheet and hang it on the wall right near the exit door.

Ask each person to fill out the survey before they leave. Reinforce that this is anonymous. You may need to leave the room if people seem shy or reluctant.

The next morning, post the completed survey and discuss it. You might ask:

> *"According to the ratings, what's going okay so far?"*
>
> *"What requires improvement?"*
>
> *"What can we do to improve?"*

Listen carefully to all suggestions. Get people to comment on each other's ideas. Write the best ideas on a flipchart and make sure that these suggestions are implemented immediately.

Team Launch Exit Survey

Explain to the team members, the following:

On your way out the door, please provide your anonymous rating of each of the four areas below. Place an X along the line to indicate where you think you are right now. We'll discuss the ratings at the next session.

1. Clarity about the team

1	2	3	4	5
Still in the dark		Somewhat confused		Feel well briefed!

2. Clarity about my role

1	2	3	4	5
Still have a lot of questions	Some questions remain			Understand my role

3. Comfort with the team goal

1	2	3	4	5
Uncomfortable		Slight discomfort		Comfortable

4. Feelings about being on the team

1	2	3	4	5
I'd rather not		Some reservations		Glad

Exit Survey for all Other Meetings

At the end of any workshop or meeting, you can copy the questions outlined in the *Generic Exit Survey* (p. 163) onto a flipchart sheet and hang it on the wall right near the door.

Ask each person to rate the meeting so far, before they leave. Reinforce that this is anonymous. You may need to leave the room if people seem shy or reluctant.

At the start of the next session, post the completed survey and discuss it. You might ask:

> *"According to the ratings, what's going okay so far?"*
>
> *"What requires improvement?"*
>
> *"What can we do to improve?"*

Listen carefully to all suggestions. Get people to comment on each other's ideas. Write the best ideas on a flipchart and make sure that these suggestions are implemented.

Generic Exit Survey

On your way out the door, please provide your anonymous rating of each of the four areas below. Place an X along the line to indicate where you think you are right now. We'll discuss the ratings once you return.

---

1. Clarity about the purpose of this meeting

1	2	3	4	5
I'm confused		I'm somewhat confused		I'm very clear

2. Pace

1	2	3	4	5
Far too slow		Just right		Felt rushed!

3. Progress

1	2	3	4	5
Achieving little		Some progress		Great progress

4. Participation

1	2	3	4	5
A few dominate		Some imbalance		Equal voices

Force Field Analysis

A Force Field Analysis is a simple tool for identifying both what is working and what isn't working for a product, process, or service. Here are the steps:

Draw the diagram below on a flipchart:

1. Focus/Topic:		
2. What's working?	**3. What's not working?**	**4. Rank order**

1. Make sure everyone is clear about exactly what's being discussed. You could do a Force Field Analysis about how a particular...

- Customer has been served in the past,
- Product has been managed,
- Process has worked in the past.

Write the focus at the top of the flipchart.

2. Ask members to tell you what has been working in terms of the focus. Ask:

> *"What is working well so far?"*
> *"What are the strengths of the current situation?"*

Record key points on the flipchart.

3. Ask members to describe *"What hasn't been working? What have the flaws been? What has gone wrong?"* Wherever possible, probe past the symptoms to get to root causes. Make sure all points are discussed at length and understood by all. Record each key point.

4. Tell members that this team can't work to fix all of the things that are wrong at once and that priorities need to be identified. The team needs to prioritize which of the items that aren't working need to be resolved and fixed the quickest. Give each person ten points and ask them to distribute these points to their top priorities. Invite members to mill at the flipchart to place their points beside the items in the "Rank order" column that most need to be fixed.

5. Once everyone is finished, add up all the votes to arrive at a total per item. The more points an item has, the more the team considers that item to be a priority.

6. Post the completed Force Field Analysis sheet on a wall and return to it when the team develops its objectives and action plans for next steps.

Team Effectiveness Survey

The *Team Effectiveness Survey* (pp. 166–167) is an important tool to manage the team's performance. Team surveys can be repeated periodically (i.e., every two months) as a preventative strategy. Follow the steps outlined below to conduct the survey:

1. Provide each member with a copy of the survey. Allow about ten minutes for each person to respond to the questions by themselves. While they do this, you should write the ten headings and the numbers one through seven under each heading, on a flipchart. Turn the flipchart toward a wall.

2. As people finish, ask them to go to the flipchart, one at a time, to record their ratings. If people are reluctant to do this, have them choose a neutral person to collect the surveys and ask that person to compile all the results onto the flipchart.

3. Turn the flipchart around once all the ratings have been recorded and review the scores. Ask members to identify all the items that they interpret to be okay. To be okay, there shouldn't be any ratings below a four for that item. List the items that received positive ratings on a flipchart sheet.

4. Identify those items that received a "below four" rating. Be aware that if even one person rated something as a one or two, that item is a problem and should be discussed.

5. Once all of the problem areas are listed, you can:

   • Discuss each with the whole group if there are only a few problems and people seem open and comfortable,

   • Write each problem item on a separate flipchart sheet. Post these sheets around the room. Let people distribute themselves into small subgroups to discuss the issue they feel they have some insight into. Have the subgroups report back to the whole group after about fifteen minutes.

Regardless of which of the above approaches is chosen, discuss two questions:

1. *"Why did this item get a low rating? (What is the problem?)"*

2. *"What can we do to rectify this situation?"*

You will notice that the proposed solutions will take the form of either action steps or new norms for the team to add to its team rules. This activity is called a *survey-feedback exercise* and always ends with the team taking responsibility for improving its own operations.

Team Effectiveness Survey

Instructions: Look over each of the following performance issues in regard to this team. Respond to each honestly, from your personal perspective. All ratings are anonymous. Priority issues to work on will be the team's lowest scored items.

1. Goal Clarity

1	2	3	4	5	6	7

Goals and objectives aren't known, understood, or accepted

Goals are clear and accepted

2. Participation

1	2	3	4	5	6	7

A few people tend to dominate

Everyone is active and has a say

3. Procedures

1	2	3	4	5	6	7

There is little structure and we lack procedures

The team has clear rules and procedures

4. Listening and Supporting

1	2	3	4	5	6	7

No one listens or provides support for each other's ideas

There is a lot of listening and building on each other's ideas

5. Confronting Difficulties

1	2	3	4	5	6	7

Conflict is avoided

Problems are identified and addressed

6. Openness and Trust

1	2	3	4	5	6	7

People seem guarded and hide their feelings

People seem open and speak freely

Team Effectiveness Survey, cont'd

7. Support

1	2	3	4	5	6	7

Little evidence of support; few offers of help — People seem ready to help and understand

8. Planning and Coordination

1	2	3	4	5	6	7

Hard to know what is happening or who is involved — Clear action steps that spell out details

9. Meetings

1	2	3	4	5	6	7

Waste of time — Well planned and productive

10. Fun

1	2	3	4	5	6	7

It's a downer — This is great!

Peer Review

About every six to eight weeks the members of any team should share feedback with each other. This is a very important preventative strategy. It lets members surface concerns with each other in a safe environment, before destructive conflict arises. Peer feedback also makes your life as leader easier because the members are coaching each other regarding their behavior and how they interrelate. Remember to include yourself in this exercise.

The feedback format provided on the following page consists of two areas of inquiry – both of which are positive. These are:

1. What you do that is really effective… (Keep on doing it!)

2. What you could do that would make you even more effective…

The first is positive because it lets people praise each other. The second is positive because it offers supportive advice to help the other person improve. The process for running this exercise consists of these steps:

1. Each member writes their name on the top of a peer feedback sheet, then passes it to the person on their right.

2. Each member answers both questions about the person whose name is at the top of each sheet.

3. Sheets are passed around the table until everyone has written their comments about each member.

4. Each person eventually gets back a completely filled sheet with comments from all of the other members.

5. Further optional steps include:

    a. Each person simply keeps their feedback to themselves.

    b. The completed sheets can be passed around again; this time each person reads out loud only the positive comments that they wrote about the other person. This is called a *strength bombardment*.

    c. Each person chooses a partner with whom they discuss their feedback. They discuss what they learned from their feedback and create action plans for personal change. Members then share their action steps with the whole group.

Peer Review Format

Name of the person receiving feedback:_____

_____

What you do that is really effective... (Keep on doing it!)

_____

What you could do that would make you even more effective...

Team Launch Evaluation Form

Instructions: Look over each of the following questions about our team launch meeting. Answer each honestly, from your personal perspective. All ratings are anonymous, although we will tabulate the results and share them to improve any items that receive a low score.

Please provide your anonymous feedback about the team launch meeting.

1. What did you like most about it? What were the most useful aspects for you personally? Describe what was positive and why.

2. What did you least like about it? What aspects were poorly run, a waste of time, etc.? Describe what was wrong and why.

3. What feedback would you like to provide to the team leader concerning how the team launch meeting was run?

4. Give your overall rating of the session.

1	2	3	4	5
Poor	Fair	Satisfactory	Good	Excellent

Additional comments/questions you still need answered:

Other Books on Team Leadership

Chang, R. 1994. *Building a Dynamic Team.*
Irvine, CA: Richard Chang Associates.

Hicks, R. and D. Bone. 1990. *Self-Managing Teams.*
Los Altos, CA: Crisp Publications.

Katzenbach, J.R. and D.K. Smith. 1993. *The Wisdom of Teams.*
New York, NY: Harper Collins.

Quick, T. 1992. *Successful Team Building.*
New York, NY: American Management Association.

Maddux, R. 1986. *Team Building: An Exercise in Leadership.*
Los Altos, CA: Crisp Publications.

Rees, F. 1991. *How to Lead Work Teams.*
San Diego, CA: Pfeiffer & Company.

Rollo, J. 1995. *Self-Directed Work Teams.*
Sarasota, FL: Competitive Advantage Consultants, Inc.

Schonk, J. 1992. *Team-Based Organizations.*
Homewood, IL: Irwin Publishing.

Torres, C. and J. Spiegel. 1990. *Self-Directed Work Teams: A Primer.*
San Diego, CA: University Associates Inc.

Reddy, W. B. 1988. *Team Building: Blueprints for Productivity & Satisfaction.*
Alexandria, VA: NTL Institute.

Wellins, R.S., W.C. Byham, and J.M. Wilson. 1991. *Empowered Teams.*
San Francisco, CA: Jossey-Bass Inc.

Wilson J.M. and J.A. George. 1994. *Team Leader's Survival Guide.*
Pittsburgh, PA: Development Dimensions International.

Bibliography

Bennis, W. and others. 1979. *Essays in Interpersonal Dynamics.* Homewood, IL: Dorsey Press.

Bennis, W. and H. Shepard. 1956. "A Theory of Group Development. " *Human Relations.*

Belasco, J. and R. Stayer. 1993. *Flight of the Buffalo.* New York, NY: Warner Books.

Block, P. 1990. *The Empowered Manager.* San Francisco, CA: Jossey-Bass.

Buchholz, S. and T. Roth. 1987. *Creating the High Performance Team.* New York, NY: John Wiley.

Byham, W.C. and J. Cox. 1988. *Zapp! The Lightning of Empowerment.* New York, NY: Ballantine Books.

Dyer, W.G. 1977. *Team Building: Issues and Alternatives.* Reading, MA: Addison-Wesley.

Dyer, W. G. 1987. *Team Building.* 2d ed. Reading, MA: Addison-Wesley.

Carr, C. 1996. *Team Leader's Problem Solver.* Upper Saddle River, NJ: Prentice Hall.

Hargrove, R. 1995. *Masterful Coaching.* San Diego, CA: Pfeiffer & Company.

Katzenbach, J. and D. Smith. 1993. *The Wisdom of Teams.* New York, NY: Harper Collins.

Kaufman, R. 1976. *Identifying and Solving Problems.* San Diego, CA: University Associates.

Kouzes, J. and B. Posner. 1987. *The Leadership Challenge.* San Francisco, CA: Jossey-Bass.

Lawler, E.E. 1986. *High Involvement Managment.* San Francisco, CA: Jossey-Bass.

Leigh, A. and M. Maynard. 1995. *Leading Your Team.* London: Nicholas Brealey Publishing.

Locke, E. and G. Latham. 1984. *Goal Setting.* Englewood Cliffs, NJ: Prentice Hall.

Luft, J. 1963. *Group Processes: An Introduction to Group Dynamics.* Palo Alto, CA: National Press.

Parker, G. and A. Brache. 1990. *Players and Teamwork.* San Francisco, CA: Jossey-Bass.

Reddy, W. B., ed. 1988. *Team Building: Blueprints for Productivity and Satisfaction.* Alexandria, VA: NTL Institute.

Rees, F. 1991. *How to Lead Work Teams: Facilitation Skills.* San Francisco, CA: Pfeiffer & Company.

Shonk, J.H. 1992. *Team-Based Organizations.* New York, NY: Irwin Professional Publishing.

Tannenbaum, R. and W. Schmidt. 1958. "How to Choose a Leadership Pattern." *Harvard Business Review.*

Tuckman, B.W. 1965. "Developmental Sequence in Small Groups." *Psychological Bulletin.*

Vroom, V.H. and P.W Yetton. 1973. *Leadership and Decision Making.* Pittsburgh, PA: University of Pittsburgh Press.

Weisbord, M.M. 1991. *Productive Workplaces.* San Francisco, CA: Jossey-Bass.

Wellins, R.S., W.C. Byham, and J.M. Wilson. 1991. *Empowered Teams,* San Francisco, CA: Jossey-Bass.

About the Author

Ingrid Bens is a consultant and trainer whose primary areas of focus are employee participation, team building, facilitation skills, leadership, and organizational change. As a facilitator she has designed and managed strategic interventions such as team formation and improvement, vision and values setting, problem solving and decision making, action planning, and troubleshooting. Ingrid has led change management and teaming projects in large companies such as General Electric, as well as in manufacturing plants, major banks, and government departments.

Ingrid has a Master's Degree in Adult Education and more than twenty years of experience as a workshop leader and organization development consultant.

About GOAL/QPC

GOAL/QPC offers products and services that provide people with the tools and methods they need to reach organizational excellence. Our leading product line, The Memory Jogger™ series of pocket guides, covers planning and quality improvement, problem solving, ISO standards, project management, teamwork, and creativity. These low-cost books can help everyone plan, work, and innovate more effectively.

Facilitation is a core skill needed for all improvement efforts. Our *Facilitation* series can help everyone improve their meeting, team, and team leadership skills — speeding the journey to excellence.

Other Available Resources on Team Building and Facilitation Offered by GOAL/QPC

Facilitating with Ease!
A comprehensive guide to the practice of facilitation. Helps build skills in managing conflict, building consensus, listening, and running effective meetings. A great resource that's easy to read, yet full of helpful strategies, tools, and worksheets. **Code: 4286P**.

Facilitation at a Glance!
A condensed, pocket-sized version of the popular manual *Facilitating with Ease!* This guide contains all the tools, techniques, and checklists you need to facilitate meetings. **Code: 1062E**.

Advanced Team Facilitation
A full-sized manual to help team leaders get their teams back on track. A great guide to help build and maintain high-level team performance. Available in spiral bound **(Code: 1036S)** and paperback **(Code: 1036P)**.

Facilitation Dynamics Video Series
Video-based series that is used as a complete learning package showing the techniques of facilitation in action. **Code: 5220**. (Additional guidebooks sold separately.)

Notes

Notes

Notes